SPECTRUM WRITING

CONTENTS

Project Editor: Sandra Kelley
Text: Written by Duncan Searl
     Design and Production by A Good Thing, Inc.
     Illustrated by Claudia Fouse, Karen Pietrobono, Doug Cushman,
         Sally Springer, John DeSoto

 Children's Publishing

Columbus, Ohio

Things To Remember About Writing

WRITING

- State the main idea of a paragraph in a topic sentence and use details to tell about the main idea.
- Write directions, recipes, and jokes in proper sequence.
- Use metaphors and similes to make your writing clearer and more colorful.
- Use details to help you write a good description.
- Base your opinions on facts to make them more convincing.
- Use a series of cause sentences and effect sentences when telling what happened in a story.
- Know your purpose and audience before you begin to write.
- Before you write, decide on your point of view and the best form to use to express that point of view.

REVISING

- Use words that are exact to make your writing more interesting.
- Use conjuctions to combine short, choppy sentences into longer, smoother sentences.
- Add or change modifiers. Be careful about their placement in your sentences.

PROOFREADING

Check to see that you have
- used capital letters correctly
- used punctuation marks correctly
- written quotations correctly
- used correct verb forms
- placed modifiers correctly

 Children's Publishing

Copyright © 2003 McGraw-Hill Children's Publishing.

Printed in the United States of America. All rights reserved. Except as permitted under the United States Copyright Act, no part of this publication may be reproduced or distributed in any form or by any means, or stored in a database retrieval system, without prior written permission from the publisher.

Send all inquiries to:
McGraw-Hill Children's Publishing
8787 Orion Place
Columbus, Ohio 43240-4027

ISBN 1-56189-935-6
2 3 4 5 6 7 8 9 10 VHG 06 05 04 03

unit 1
Writing Main Ideas

Things to Remember About Using Main Ideas in Your Writing

The **main idea** of a paragraph is what the paragraph is all about.

Writing Tips

- State the main idea of a paragraph in a topic sentence.
- Use details in the paragraph to tell about the main idea.
- Have all the sentences in a paragraph tell about the main idea of the paragraph so that the idea is clear.
- Keep your topic narrow enough for one paragraph.
- Use examples and other details to develop your topic.

Revising Tips

- Use exact nouns to make your writing more interesting and accurate.

Proofreading Tips

Check to see that every sentence
- has a subject and a verb
- begins with a capital letter
- ends with a period, an exclamation point, or a question mark.

1 Writing topic sentences

Look at this picture.

What is the main idea of the picture? You might say that one fisherman caught a lot of fish but the other pulled up a rubber tire.

Paragraphs also have main ideas. The **main idea** of a paragraph is what the paragraph is all about. The **details** in the paragraph tell about the main idea.

A. Write a paragraph about the picture above. You already know the main idea. Add some details to complete your paragraph.

_____

_____

_____

_____

_____

Sometimes the main idea is stated in one sentence. This sentence is called the **topic sentence.** The topic sentence can be found anywhere in a paragraph, but usually it comes at the beginning or end of the paragraph. Do you have a topic sentence in your paragraph for part **A**? If so, underline it.

B. Read the following paragraph. Underline the topic sentence.

Either the well was very deep, or Alice fell very slowly, for she had plenty of time as she went down to look about her and to wonder what was going to happen next. First, she tried to look down and make out what she was coming to, but it was too dark to see anything. Then she looked at the sides of the well and noticed that they were filled with cupboards and bookshelves. She took down a jar from one of the shelves as she passed. It was labeled "ORANGE MARMALADE," but to her great disappointment it was empty. She did not like to drop the jar for fear of killing somebody underneath, so she managed to put it into one of the cupboards as she fell past it.

—*Lewis Carroll*

C. Read the following paragraph. Think about the details. Think about what the whole paragraph is about. Then write a topic sentence below.

Last Thursday, strange tracks were found in Clancy's farm. On Friday, Maybelle Henning claims she saw a huge, apelike creature on Route 12D, near Ludlow. Something ripped the door off Tony Alfa's chicken coop and ate nineteen chickens Sunday morning. Today, Mayor Rodriguez says he saw an apeman with a sheep under its arm near Blanket Lake.

_____

_____

On another sheet of paper, write a paragraph about the strangest thing you have ever seen. Experiment with where you place the topic sentence. Write the paragraph in three different ways. First, begin with the topic sentence. Next, end with the topic sentence. Finally, rewrite the paragraph with the topic sentence in the middle of the paragraph.

The topic sentence states the main idea of a paragraph. The details tell about the main idea.

lesson 2 Keeping to the topic

Cynthia is going to a Halloween party. If she wants to dress as Captain Hook, she has to choose the details of her costume carefully. An eye patch and an old three-cornered hat will do. A fancy dress is out of place.

Paragraphs should be dressed properly too. Make sure all the details in your sentences fit the main idea.

A. What would you wear if you were going to a Halloween party? Write a topic sentence about your costume. Then add details to describe each part of the costume.

_____

_____

_____

_____

_____

_____

B. Read the following paragraphs. Underline the topic sentence in each. Cross out any sentences that don't tell about the topic. Then write another sentence about the main idea on the lines after each paragraph.

The food at Mrs. Roald's picnic was spectacular! Giant hams, huge steaming roast beefs, and mountains of fried chicken were piled high on one long table. Everyone played softball, and there were pony rides for the kids. I've never seen so many salads—potato, garden fruit, and about twelve others I didn't recognize. I once got sick from eating egg salad.

_____

_____

People's body language, or the way they move, can show how they are feeling. For example, I always drum my fingers on the nearest desk or chair when I'm bored. My friend Sophie twists a strand of her hair when she's nervous. She has nice dark hair that she wears long. I like my hair short. My dad folds his arms and clears his throat when he's getting angry.

_____

_____

On a separate sheet, write a topic sentence. Choose one of those listed below or think of your own. Then write a paragraph in which each detail sentence tells about the topic.

I think dogs make the best pets.
There was one day in my life that I'd like to forget.
What an exciting game we had!

All the sentences in a paragraph should tell about the main idea of the paragraph.

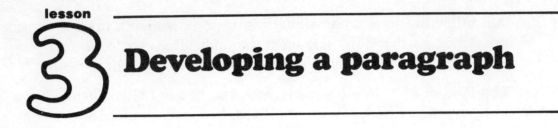

lesson 3 Developing a paragraph

How would you complete this paragraph?

There are lots of things I like about life.

This idea is too big to develop in one paragraph. A good writer **narrows** the main idea to a topic that can be developed in one paragraph. For example:

There are certain things I like about living next to a restaurant.

A. List some details that could go with this topic sentence.

_____

_____

_____

_____

B. The following topic sentences are much too broad to develop in a paragraph. Rewrite them so that they are more narrow.

1. I've been thinking about things a lot lately.

_____

_____

2. People do very unusual things.

_____

_____

When writing about your ideas and feelings, often the best kinds of details are **examples.** One good example will illustrate a main idea better than many sentences of explanation. For example, instead of saying "I was very unhappy," you might say, "Every night I sobbed into my pillow until it was too soggy to sleep on."

C. A topic sentence is given below. Write a paragraph to go with it. Remember to use sentences that give examples or other details about the topic sentence.

Joe's Uncle Englebert is a real character. _____

_____

_____

_____

_____

_____

_____

On another sheet of paper, write an idea for a script that will be used for one story of your favorite TV series. In one sentence briefly state the main idea of the show. Then write a paragraph about your script which develops the main idea by adding examples and other details.

Before you develop a paragraph, be sure your topic is narrow enough. You can develop your topic by giving examples and other details.

Writing a science paragraph

Pretend you wake up one morning and decide to think like a scientist. There has been a snowstorm the night before, and you form the idea that many people and animals have already enjoyed the snow in the park across the street. What do you do to prove your idea? You go to the window and observe the following patterns of tracks.

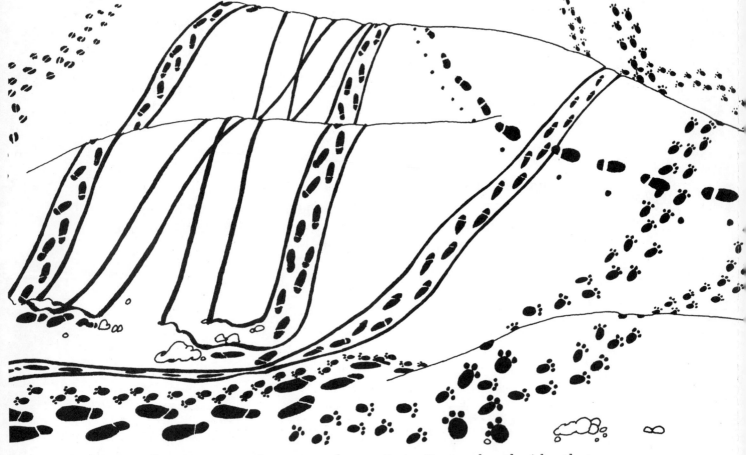

A. Write a few sentences about your observations. Remember the idea that you want to prove.

_____

_____

_____

_____

_____

_____

Scientists observe. They write down **facts** about what they observe. Then they draw **conclusions** based on their observations.

B. Some scientists study objects from the past to learn how they were used and who used them. Below are three pictures of objects from the past. Choose one and study it carefully. Then draw some conclusions about what it was used for and who used it. On the lines below, write your conclusions and the facts you based them on.

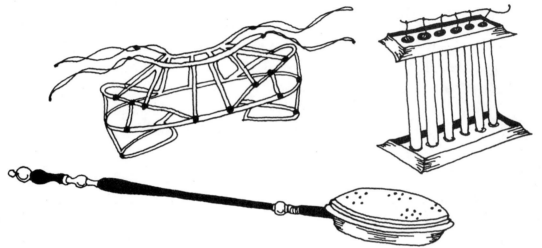

_____

_____

_____

_____

Scientific discoveries often make new inventions possible. If you were a scientist, what would you like to invent? A machine to get you out of bed and dress you? A jet-propelled bike? A homework machine? On another sheet of paper, state the main idea of your invention: what it is and what it does. Then describe your invention in more detail. Write clear sentences. Draw a picture of your invention if you wish.

_____

Science paragraphs should contain facts and conclusions.

5 Writing a social studies paragraph

How is a social studies paragraph like a newspaper article? They both usually answer *wh* questions: **who, what, where, when,** and **why.** Often the topic sentence answers most of these questions.

A. Read the following paragraphs. Write answers to the questions on the lines below.

1. George McJunkin, a black cowboy, made a great discovery in 1925. He spotted some unusual animal bones in the dry bed of a stream near Folsom, New Mexico. He also found a graceful stone spearhead among the bones. The spear had killed the animal.

Who: _____

When: _____

Where: _____

What: _____

2. News of McJunkin's find reached some scientists at a nearby university. The scientists were very surprised when they investigated the find. The bones were of a type of buffalo that had been extinct for eight thousand years. Since only humans can make spearheads, the scientists realized that people had been in America at least eight thousand years ago. This was much earlier than anyone had thought.

Who: _____

What: _____

Why: _____

B. Use the following information to write a short paragraph about the first women's rights convention in the U.S. Be sure to include a topic sentence.

Who: Elizabeth Cady Stanton and Lucretia Mott
When: 1848
Where: Seneca Falls, New York
What: small meeting
Why: to work for women's right to vote

_____

_____

_____

_____

_____

Social studies paragraphs present facts that answer *wh* questions. People who read and write social studies, however, are also interested in the explanation of facts. Choose one of the facts below to explain on another piece of paper. Tell how the fact has changed the way of life of your community, your family, or yourself.

In 1920, the Nineteenth Amendment gave women the right to vote.
In 1903, the Wright Brothers flew an engine-driven airplane for the first time.
By 1951, television programs were broadcast from coast to coast.

Social studies paragraphs answer the questions <u>who</u>, <u>what</u>, <u>where</u>, <u>when</u>, and <u>why</u>. Social studies paragraphs also explain facts.

Revising

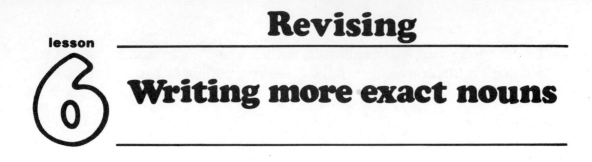

6 Writing more exact nouns

What's wrong with the ad below?

Well, a boat can be a beautiful new ocean liner or a dumpy old rowboat. Before you pay five hundred dollars, you'd probably want to know exactly what kind of boat you'd be traveling on. A more **exact noun,** like *rowboat,* gives more information than a general noun, like *boat.*

A. Read the following sentences. Replace each underlined general noun by writing an exact noun on the lines. You can use your own exact noun or choose one from the list below.

Saint Bernard   sports car   shriek
fruit salad   daisies

1. The <u>animal</u> saved the little girl's life by keeping her warm during the

   snowstorm. _____

2. The field shimmered with <u>flowers</u>. _____

3. That <u>food</u> sure tasted good. _____

4. Suddenly a <u>sound</u> rang out in the night. _____

5. Ted drove up in his new <u>vehicle</u>. _____

B. For every general noun below, write two more exact nouns.

1. animal   _____   _____

2. clothes   _____   _____

3. furniture   _____   _____

4. snack   _____   _____

5. feeling   _____   _____

C. Rewrite the following paragraph. Replace each underlined noun or noun phrase with a more exact noun or noun phrase.

These two <u>guys</u> went hiking one day. <u>One guy</u> walked into <u>this place</u> and saw <u>this thing</u> peering through the trees. They just stared at each other for <u>some time</u>. <u>The other guy</u> dropped his <u>stuff</u> and took off. <u>The first guy</u> jumped and screamed, and <u>another person</u> came and scared it away.

_____

_____

_____

_____

_____

Look over all the "Write On" paragraphs you've written for this unit. Pay special attention to the nouns. Choose one paragraph that could use more exact nouns. Rewrite it. Make sure the nouns you choose name exactly what you have in mind.

Use exact nouns to make your writing more interesting and accurate.

Proofreading

Writing complete sentences

lesson 7

Look at the word groups below.

1	2
Kristie walked	Robin ran
3	4
crawled outside	Robin at the store

A. Write answers to the questions below.

1. Which word groups—1, 2, 3, and/or 4—would you say are complete sentences? _____

2. Which word groups are not complete sentences? _____

3. What are the subjects in word groups 1 and 2?

   _____   _____

4. What are the verbs in word groups 1 and 2?

   _____   _____

5. Does word group 3 contain a subject? _____

6. Does word group 4 contain a verb? _____

B. Think about how you answered the questions for part **A**. What two parts must a complete sentence have?

   _____   _____

C. Read the following word groups. Write an S next to each complete sentence. Write an N next to each word group that is not a complete sentence.

1. Hazel cooks _____

2. Walter the desk _____

3. The orange, red, and yellow flame _____

14

4. He walked quietly down the hill _____

5. Looking carefully through _____

6. The rain fell _____

7. Going to the fair _____

8. Lois jumped, and I yelled _____

9. He and the rhinoceros _____

10. The greatest day _____

A sentence begins with a capital letter and ends with a period, an exclamation point, or a question mark. Study these sentences.

Bruce nodded his head. His eyes closed slowly. Soon he was asleep.

The sentences above have been proofread. **Proofreading** means reading over what you have written and making corrections. Notice how the corrections above were made.

D. Proofread and correct the sentences below.

The cook stirred the mixture then he poured it into a baking dish

He it into the oven. When do think it will be ready.

As you proofread your writing, check to see:
- **that every sentence has a subject and a verb**
- **that every sentence begins with a capital letter**
- **that every sentence ends with a period, an exclamation point, or a question mark**

Post-Test

1. Underline the more exact noun in each pair below.

    a. ballplayer/catcher   e. schooner/sailboat

    b. apricot/fruit   f. collie/dog

    c. descendant/grandson   g. vegetable/eggplant

    d. cat/leopard   h. pliers/tool

2. Read the paragraph below. Underline the topic sentence and cross out the sentence that doesn't fit the topic.

    There are several stories about how May was named. The most widely accepted one is that it was named for Maia, the Roman goddess of spring and growth. Diana is the Roman goddess of hunting. But some people say that May is short for *majores*, the Latin word for "older men." They believe that May was the month dedicated to the majores, just as June was dedicated to *juniores* (young men).

3. Proofread and correct the sentences below.

    The hum of a mosquito is the sound of its wings beating a mosquito's wings move about a thousand times a second. A female's wings a higher tone than a male's wings. Why is that. Helps males find mates.

4. Choose one sentence below. Revise it to make the underlined noun more specific. Then use your new sentence as the main idea for a paragraph. Write your paragraph on a separate piece of paper.

    A <u>person</u> is important in our community.

    A <u>thing</u> is my most prized possession.

    I would like to live in a <u>place</u>.

16

unit 2
Writing in Sequence

Things to Remember About Writing in Sequence

Sequence tells what comes first, next, and last.

Writing Tips

- Use sequence words like *first, next, then,* and *last* to show the order of events.
- Write directions, recipes, and jokes in proper sequence.
- Use directional words like *north* or *left* when writing directions.
- Use an outline to keep your information and paragraphs in sequence when you write.

Revising Tips

- Use exact verbs to make your writing more interesting and accurate.

Proofreading Tips Check that you have

- begun each important word of a proper noun with a capital letter

1 Writing instructions in sequence

This house painter wants to paint the trim on the roof. However, she has a little problem—she left out an important step. What is it?

She forgot to bring the bucket of paint with her when she climbed the ladder.

In order to do anything—paint a house or brush your teeth—you have to perform a number of steps in the right **sequence,** or order.

A. Here is a list of steps for making papier-mâché. They are not in the correct sequence. Put them in the correct sequence on the lines below.

1. Dip the strips of newspaper into the mixture.
2. Apply the strips to the form.
3. Stir until the mixture is smooth, sticky, and wet.
4. Mix two parts water with one part flour.

First: _____

Next: _____

Third: _____

Finally: _____

B. On the next page, write instructions for doing one of the following: blowing up a balloon; giving a dog a bath; making an ice-cream soda.

How to _____

First: _____

Next: _____

Third: _____

Finally: _____

C. Read the following instructions.

How Not to Paint the Floor

1. Begin painting at the doorway and work your way into the room.
2. Paint around the furniture that is too heavy to move.
3. After painting one third of the room, sweep and wash the rest of the floor.
4. After you've painted yourself into a corner, walk across the floor and leave the room.

Now rewrite these instructions. Tell how one should really go about painting a floor. Use **sequence words** like _first_, _next_, _then_, and _last_.

_____

_____

_____

_____

_____

_____

You can probably do at least one of the activities below without thinking twice. But can you write instructions on how to do it? Instructions have to be in a clear, step-by-step sequence. Write your instructions on a separate sheet of paper.

building a paper airplane   playing hopscotch
doing a cartwheel   diving from a diving board

Instructions should be written in sequence. Sequence words like <u>first</u>, <u>next</u>, <u>then</u>, and <u>last</u> help show the order.

2 Writing directions in sequence

Did you ever get lost because someone gave you mixed-up directions? Good directions have to be given in clear, step-by-step sequence.

A. Look at the map. Using complete sentences, write directions on the lines below that tell Kermit how he can bicycle to his friends' campsite. Use sequence words and clear **directional words** like *north* or *east*, *left* or *right*.

_____

_____

_____

_____

_____

20

B. Holly Miyamoto was a prisoner at Uln on Radex 23, a planet 23 million light-years from Earth. She escaped and made her way to the Gabriel Space Shuttle. Look at the map below. Then, using complete sentences, write a description of her escape route on the lines that follow. Be sure to write your description in sequence. Begin with Uln. Use the compass whenever possible.

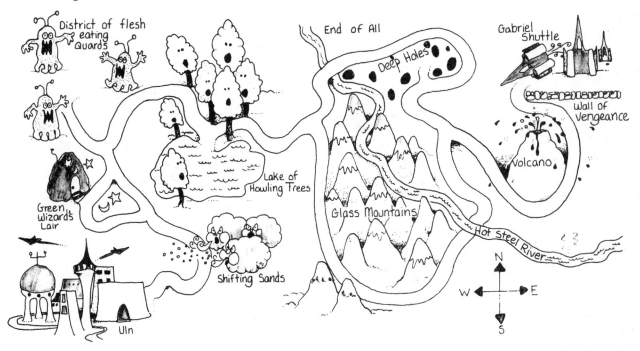

_____

_____

_____

_____

_____

 What happened to Holly when she passed the Shifting Sands, the Green Wizard's Lair, or the Lake of Howling Trees? On another sheet of paper, write a story about some of Holly's adventures as she escaped from Uln. Write your story in sequence and use some of the directions you have written for part **B.** Your story should be at least ten sentences long, but it can be longer.

Always write directions in sequence.

Writing a recipe

Meet Julia Chicken, world-famous cook and television star. She's preparing one of her very special dishes.

Perhaps Julia should be a bit more careful about following the recipe directions in sequence.

A. Read the following recipe for preparing pumpkin seeds. Number the steps in the correct sequence.

_____ Bake them for five minutes at 500 degrees.

_____ Cut open a pumpkin.

_____ Pull the seeds out of the pumpkin.

_____ Let them cool.

_____ Rinse the pulp off the seeds with cold water.

_____ Spread the seeds on a cookie sheet and sprinkle salt on them.

_____ Eat!

B. How clever are you in the kitchen? On the next page is a list of ingredients and equipment for a good, old-fashioned stew. Write your own recipe for the stew. Add a few more ingredients if you wish. Give your stew a name.

Ingredients	Equipment
½ tank car oil	1 dirty gym sock
2 toad's eyes	1 wash bucket
¼ teaspoon of ant's eggs	1 table tennis paddle
ooze from a rotten eggplant	
milkweed juice	
4 or 5 wasp pods	

_____

_____

_____

_____

_____

C. Pretend you are making a salad for a visitor from outer space. He wants to take the recipe back to Mars with him. On the following lines, write the directions for making your favorite salad. If you don't like salad, write the recipe for a dessert.

_____

_____

_____

_____

_____

 If you've finished all the activities in this lesson, you should be a pretty good cook. Prepare a dream dinner. On another sheet of paper, write a menu for your perfect meal. Include a recipe for one dream dish.

Write recipes in sequence.

Writing jokes

What makes a joke funny? A joke is a story that is told or written in careful sequence. It usually leads up to a surprising, funny ending called the **punch line.** Read the comic strip below. Pay attention to its sequence.

A. Can you tell the joke on page 24 entirely in words? Write a paragraph about it. Be sure to write the joke in the correct sequence. Using sequence words like *then* and *finally* can help keep the order clear.

_____

_____

_____

_____

_____

_____

B. If you put the following sentences in sequence, you will get another joke. Number the sentences in sequence. Then write them in a paragraph.

_____ She takes a sip and screams, "This coffee tastes like mud."

_____ A woman goes into a diner and orders a cup of coffee.

_____ The waiter says, "Well, it was ground this morning."

_____ Hey, did you ever hear this one?

_____

_____

_____

_____

 Write your own favorite joke. A funny punch line has to come as a surprise, so make sure your joke leads up to it carefully.

_____

Jokes should be written or told in sequence.

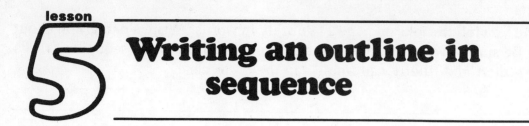

Writing an outline in sequence

Outlining is a good way to keep your information and paragraphs in sequence when you are writing. If you outline, you can plot the sequence before you write. This makes the job of writing much easier. For example, if you were going to write about Harry Houdini, the great magician, you might set up an outline in the following sequence.

Harry Houdini
I. Childhood
  A. Life at home
  B. Life as a boy in the circus
II. Adulthood
  A. As a trapeze artist
  B. As a magician

A. Below is some information about the Abominable Snowman. List each fact under the proper heading in the outline that follows.

> Lives in Mount Everest and other Himalaya mountains
> Hairy body and face like person
> In 1951, a British explorer took pictures of "snowman" tracks
> The beast may simply be a large bear
> Walks erect on thick legs
> When bear tracks in snow melt, they may look like huge footprints
> Sometimes seen near villages
> Several expeditions have searched for the beast

The Abominable Snowman
I. What is it?
  A. Appearance

  1. _____

  2. _____
  B. Where it is found

  1. _____

  2. _____

II. Does it really exist?
   A. Expeditions

      1. _____

      2. _____
   B. Explanations

      1. _____

      2. _____

B. Make an outline of what happened to you last year. The four seasons can serve as main headings. The events that occurred will be subheads.

  I. Winter

    A. _____

    B. _____

 II. Spring

    A. _____

    B. _____

III. Summer

    A. _____

    B. _____

IV. Autumn

    A. _____

    B. _____

 Use your outline about last year's events to write about your year. Use the headings and subheadings for topic sentences—you will need to rewrite them as complete sentences. Then write detail sentences that tell about each topic sentence.

Use an outline to plan your writing in sequence.

Revising

lesson

6

Writing with more interesting verbs

A good writer chooses verbs carefully. To express an idea well, a writer should use an **exact verb.**

A. Think of one or more verbs that could be used instead of *walked* in the following sentence to express the ideas below. The first one has been done to get you started.

The girl <u>walked</u> down the street.

1. happiness _Skipped, pranced_

2. haste _____

3. clumsiness _____

4. pain _____

5. tiredness _____

B. Write more exact verbs for the verb *said* in the following sentence to express the ideas below.

The boy <u>said</u>, "I did it."

1. loudness _____

2. sadness _____

3. softness _____

4. happiness _____

5. confusion _____

Your writing will be more interesting and more accurate if you use one exact verb instead of a general verb helped by an adverb. For example:

Butch, Slim, and I <u>walked slowly</u> past Creely's dump.
Butch, Slim, and I <u>trudged</u> past Creely's dump.

28

C. Think of one exact verb to replace the underlined verb and adverb in the sentences below.

1. "Such a dull summer," Butch <u>said unhappily</u>. _____

2. Just then Lem Moss's time machine <u>came noisily</u> into sight. _____

_____

3. Its silver and glass discs <u>shone brightly</u> in the sun. _____

4. In a second we were <u>moving quickly</u> after it. _____

5. The time machine landed on the courthouse lawn; Judge Kick was

<u>looking carefully</u> at the cockpit. _____

6. The cockpit slid open, and Lem Moss and a strange creature <u>came quickly</u>

out of the machine. _____

7. "I'm just back from the twenty-third century," Lem <u>said loudly</u>, "and do I

have news for you!" _____

Look back over the directions and recipes you wrote for this unit. Pay special attention to the verbs and verb phrases that you used. Can any of them be sharper or more exact? Choose one paragraph or essay to improve. On another sheet of paper, rewrite the paragraph or essay using more exact verbs.

_____

Use exact verbs to make your writing more interesting and accurate.

Proofreading

7

Using capital letters correctly

Proper nouns name particular people and places. Here are some proper nouns from this unit. Notice that each important word of a proper noun begins with a capital letter.

Kermit	Woodland Road	Gabriel Space Shuttle
Julia Chicken	Lake of Howling Trees	Mount Everest

A. Fill in the blanks below with proper nouns. Be sure to begin each proper noun with a capital letter.

My favorite TV star: _____

The street where I live: _____

The nicest person I know: _____

A country I'd like to see: _____

A body of water: _____

The capital of my state: _____

Names of particular days, months, businesses, and buildings also use capital letters.

Monday	March	Tower of Pisa
Labor Day	Nystrom's Market	Lafayette School

B. Proofread and correct these sentences. Put in capital letters where they are needed.

1. Did kermit ride his bike into quake lake?

2. Holly miyamoto flew to saturn last thursday.

3. I watch julia chicken every tuesday.

4. An explorer named black got lost in the painted desert.

5. We went to detroit on friday, december 1.

6. The northfield school is closed on columbus day.

7. The tower of pizza is on poplar street in newburgh.

8. Isn't jason's mart having a sale for election day?

C. Copy the paragraph below. Replace each underlined word group with a proper noun.

On <u>one day</u>, <u>a girl</u> went shopping at <u>a store</u> in <u>a city</u>. Then she met a friend at <u>a restaurant</u> on <u>a street</u>. After lunch, <u>the girl</u> and <u>her friend</u> went to <u>a museum</u>.

_____

_____

_____

_____

_____

Begin each important word of a proper noun with a capital letter. Proper nouns include names of particular people, places, days, businesses, and buildings.

Post-Test

1. Number the sentences of this joke in the correct sequence.

   a. _____ How could your horse be too polite?

   b. _____ It wasn't good because the horse was too polite.

   c. _____ How was your horseback riding yesterday, Ann?

   d. _____ Whenever we came to a fence, he let me go first.

2. Number the recipe directions so that they are in sequence.

   a. _____ Stir the water and oats mixture constantly.

   b. _____ Bring one cup of water to a rapid boil.

   c. _____ Serve with melted butter, honey, or cream.

   d. _____ Add ½ cup of Fast Oats to the boiling water.

   e. _____ Remove cereal from heat after 2½ minutes.

3. Underline the more exact verb in each pair below.
   a. move, stroll   d. chatter, talk
   b. cook, broil   e. run, dart
   c. gulp, drink   f. laugh, giggle

4. Add capital letters where they are needed in these sentences.

   a. One monday in may richard powers visited chicago, illinois.

   b. He stayed at the sheraton hotel and went to the sears tower.

5. Make an outline of what you will do this weekend. The main headings can
   be: I. Friday night; II. Saturday; III. Sunday. List your weekend plans as
   subheads in the outline. Then use your outline to write three paragraphs
   about the weekend. Be sure each paragraph has a topic sentence and detail
   sentences.

32

unit

Writing Comparisons

Things to Remember About Writing Comparisons

A **comparison** tells how things are alike or different.

Writing

- Add *er* or *more* to adjectives when you compare two things.
- Add *est* or *most* to adjectives when you compare more than two things.
- Use metaphors and similes to make your writing clearer and more colorful. Remember that a simile contains *like* or *as*. A metaphor compares without using *like* or *as*.

Revising

- Use exact adjectives to write clear descriptions.

Proofreading

Check to see that you have used commas to

- separate items in a list of three or more items
- separate two or more adjectives in place of *and*
- set off the words *yes* and *no* or the name of the person you are talking to
- separate the day from the year in a date
- separate the street, city, state, or country in an address

Using adjectives in comparisons

When we **compare** things, we look for ways in which they are similar and ways in which they are different. One way to compare different things is to tell how they look, feel, sound, smell, or taste. We use **adjectives** to make such comparisons.

A. List the adjectives from the picture above.

_____   _____

_____   _____

Notice that we change short adjectives that compare two items by adding er at the end. We use *more* in front of longer adjectives when we compare two items.

B. Write a sentence with an adjective to compare each pair below.

1. a baseball and a basketball: _____

_____

2. a flower and a weed: _____

_____

3. a pencil and a typewriter: _____

_____

When we use adjectives to compare more than two items, we add *est* to short adjectives. We use the word *most* in front of longer adjectives.

Of the three kittens, Snowball has the <u>whitest</u> fur.
But Tiger is the <u>most playful</u> of the three.

C. Choose one of the groups below. Write three or more sentences using adjectives to compare the different members of the group.

> an apple, a cherry, and a banana
> a mouse, a dog, and an elephant
> a skateboard, a bike, and a car

_____

_____

_____

_____

Think of two TV characters, two places, or two meals to compare. Choose one that you like a lot and one that you don't like. Then write a paragraph comparing the two. Try to use an *er* or *more* adjective in each sentence in your paragraph.

Add <u>er</u> or <u>more</u> to adjectives when you are comparing two things. Add <u>est</u> or <u>most</u> to adjectives when you compare more than two things.

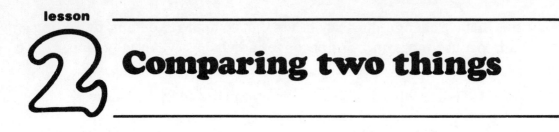

lesson 2 Comparing two things

A. The following description of a classroom was written in 1837. Read it carefully. Then, on the lines below, compare the windows, furniture, walls, and ceiling of your classroom with those in the description.

. . . a bare and dirty room, with a couple of windows, whereof a tenth part might be of glass, the remainder being stopped up with old copybooks and paper. There were a couple of long old rickety desks, cut and notched and inked and damaged in every possible way. . . . The ceiling was supported, like that of a barn, by cross beams and rafters, and the walls were so stained and discolored that it was impossible to tell whether they had ever been touched with paint or whitewash.

—*Charles Dickens*

	Dickens's Classroom	**My Classroom**
Windows	_____	_____
	_____	_____
	_____	_____
Furniture	_____	_____
	_____	_____
	_____	_____
Ceiling	_____	_____
	_____	_____
	_____	_____
Walls	_____	_____
	_____	_____
	_____	_____

B. Look at these pictures. On the lines that follow, make a list of four things which have changed about Manhattan Island and New York Harbor between 1776 and 1976.

1776	1976
1. _____	_____
_____	_____
2. _____	_____
_____	_____
3. _____	_____
_____	_____
4. _____	_____
_____	_____

There are two ways to write paragraphs comparing the pictures above. You can list how things were in 1776 in one paragraph and then, in a second paragraph, tell what things are like now. Or you can compare the pictures—point by point—in one paragraph. On another sheet of paper, write one paragraph or two paragraphs comparing the pictures.

Comparisons tell how things are alike or different.

3 Telling how things are similar

Why is a dirty person like wool?

You probably realize this question is a **riddle.** That means you must look for an unusual or funny way in which these two things might be alike. (How are they similar? Why, they both shrink from washing.)

A. Think about the following pairs of objects as if they were riddles. Name two ways that the members of each pair are alike.

1. a dictionary and a comic book

_____

_____

2. a pencil and an arrow

_____

_____

3. a balloon and a bubble

_____

_____

4. a lifetime and a journey

_____

_____

B. Look at the two pictures on page 38. On the lines that follow, write a short paragraph that states three or more ways in which the jet is similar to a condor.

_____

_____

_____

_____

_____

_____

_____

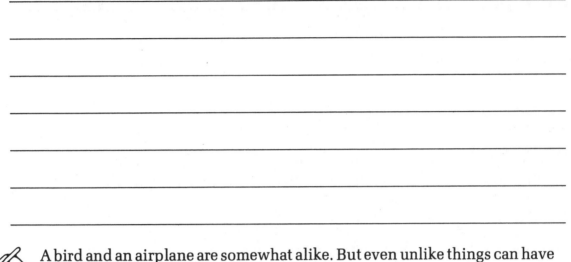 A bird and an airplane are somewhat alike. But even unlike things can have similarities. For example, you can compare ants to people by explaining how ants divide up their work into special jobs much the way people do.

Choose one of the following topic sentences. Think about ways that the two items are alike. Then, on another sheet of paper, write a paragraph comparing the two.

1. A football game is a lot like a battle.
2. In many ways, a school is like a little world.
3. Sometimes I think pet dogs and cats are like people.

You can tell how things are similar when they are a lot alike and even when they aren't.

lesson 4 Writing with similes

A **simile** is a comparison that uses the words *like* or *as*. These words clearly show that a comparison is being made.

> Anita's hair is <u>as</u> curly <u>as</u> lamb's wool.
> Cutting her hair was <u>like</u> shearing a sheep.

A. Find five similes in these lines from "A Visit from Saint Nicholas." Then on the lines below, write what is being compared in each simile.

His eyes, how they twinkled! His dimples, how merry!
His cheeks were like roses, his nose like a cherry!
And the beard on his chin was as white as the snow;
The stump of a pipe he held tight in his teeth,
And the smoke it encircled his head like a wreath;
He had a broad face and a little round belly,
That shook when he laughed like a bowl full of jelly.

—Clement Moore

1. _____ are compared to _____ .

2. _____ is compared to _____ .

3. _____ is compared to _____ .

4. _____ is compared to _____ .

5. _____ is compared to _____ .

Similes can make our spoken and written language more colorful. Frequently similes are funny or descriptive. Here are two ways to say the same thing.

He was very happy.
He was as happy as a mosquito at a crowded beach.

B. Complete the following similes. Try to think of fresh and different comparisons.

1. clumsy as _____

2. hot as _____

3. Your suit looks like _____.

4. She plays tennis as if _____.

5. as nervous as _____

6. a laugh like _____

7. He walks like _____.

C. Now write similes that describe two of the following situations. Use the lines below.

the cafeteria during lunchtime   a blizzard
waking up from a nightmare   the last day of summer vacation

_____

_____

_____

_____

The following poem is made up of similes.

My grandmother was tall, like the sunflowers near the porch.
Her eyes were gray, like the granite walls of the courthouse.
My grandmother was strong, like the tree roots which push up sidewalks.

Write your own simile poem. First, think about someone or something you have strong feelings for—a member of your family, a friend, a pet, your home. Next, decide what you will compare the person or thing with. Finally, write your comparisons in a series of similes.

A simile is a comparison that contains the words <u>like</u> or <u>as</u>. You can use similes to make your writing colorful.

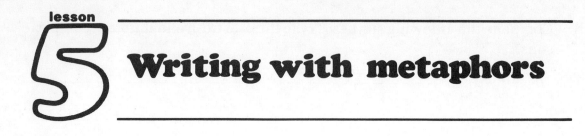

lesson 5 Writing with metaphors

A **metaphor** compares two things without using *like* or *as*. A metaphor uses a word or phrase which means one thing to describe another.

   This classroom is a zoo.
   The ghost of a moon slipped behind the trees and disappeared.

A. Tell what two things are being compared in each metaphor above.

   1. _____

   2. _____

   Metaphors can help readers see things in new ways. Metaphors add color and imagination to writing.

B. Look at the pictures below. What do they remind you of? On the lines at the top of page 43, write a metaphor to describe each picture.

42

1. _____

_____

2. _____

_____

C. What do the following things remind you of? Using metaphors, write sentences about four of the items on the lines below.

a spring day   a difficult math problem   an old, worn-out car
a stingy person   a garbage dump   an alarm clock

1. _____

_____

2. _____

_____

3. _____

_____

4. _____

_____

A metaphor can be just one sentence. Or a whole paragraph can extend the metaphor and explain it. For example:

Grace was a walking tape recorder. She was the nosiest person in the school. Her ears were microphones. She seemed to have a special sense that could pick up a piece of hot gossip at the other end of the cafeteria. She heard—and remembered—everything.

Choose one of the metaphors you wrote for part **B** or part **C,** or think of another. On a separate sheet of paper, write a paragraph that extends and explains your metaphor.

A metaphor uses one thing to describe another without using the words <u>as</u> or <u>like</u>. You can use metaphors to make your writing colorful and imaginative.

Revising

Writing more exact adjectives

A. The man in the picture just sold you a radio that doesn't work. You want to warn your friends. How would you describe the man? Jot down a few adjectives on the following lines.

_____

_____

_____

_____

You probably know that describing him as "some guy" won't help. You want to use more exact adjectives so your friends can picture him clearly in their minds. Try to use **exact adjectives** whenever you write a description.

B. Look at the pair of adjectives in each of the following sentences. Underline the more specific adjective.

1. The man had a (rasping, funny) voice.

2. He had a (weird, dangerous) look in his eye.

3. The man's jacket was (crumpled, old looking).

4. His movements were (strange, jerky).

5. His (choppy, peculiar) manner of speaking made me feel (nervous, bad).

44

C. Read the next paragraph. It's about the farmhouse in the picture on this page.

It was a nice, old farmhouse built over a pretty brook. Next to the house was a lovely meadow with fantastic flowers everywhere. The house was a wonderful building with neat little windows and doors.

We know from the sample paragraph that the writer liked the farmhouse, but we don't know what the farmhouse looked like. Rewrite the paragraph on the lines below. Look at the picture and choose exact adjectives that describe what you see.

_____

_____

_____

_____

_____

Choose one "Write On" paragraph that you've written for this unit and improve the adjectives. Make them clearer, more descriptive, and more exciting. Rewrite your paragraph on another sheet of paper.

Use exact adjectives to give clear descriptions.

Proofreading

Using commas correctly

Punctuation marks help readers understand the meaning of written sentences and paragraphs. Readers know that periods, question marks, and exclamation points signal the ends of sentences. **Commas** are used to signal pauses or slight separations between words within sentences. Look at the way these commas are used.

> I ate an apple, a cherry, and a banana.
> It was a bare, dirty classroom.

Commas separate each item in a list of three or more items. Commas also separate two or more adjectives when you can put *and* between them.

A. Put in commas where they are needed in the following sentences.

1. Janice climbed the old rickety staircase.

2. She knocked banged and pushed on the door.

3. It opened with a high squeaky sigh.

4. The bare room held only a table a chair and a saucer of milk.

5. Suddenly she saw a small skinny cat perched on the windowsill.

Commas are also used in the following ways:

1. **To set off the words <u>yes</u> and <u>no</u> or the name of the person you are talking to:**

    Yes, I'm ready.   Virginia, are you ready?

2. **To separate the day from the year in a date:**

    He was born on December 25, 1970.

3. **To separate the street, the city, and the state, province, or country in an address:**

    I live at 103 Hillcrest Avenue, Windsor, Ontario.

B. Put in commas where they are needed in the sentences below.

1. No I don't live in Oakland California.

2. Kim my new address is 95 Birch Lane Oakdale Pennsylvania.

3. I moved there on April 14 1979.

4. The package was delivered on October 9 1976.

5. Yes Bert the package came from Mexico City Mexico.

C. Proofread and correct this paragraph. Add end punctuation, commas, and capital letters where they are needed.

    yes jack I lost my wallet my money and my keys I can't get into my house

at 37 lombard street columbus ohio can you help me

When you proofread your writing, check to see that you have used commas properly. Use them:
*   **to separate each item in a list of three or more items**
*   **to separate two or more adjectives in place of <u>and</u>**
*   **to set off the words <u>yes</u> and <u>no</u> or the name of the person you are talking to**
*   **to separate the day from the year in a date**
*   **to separate the street, the city, and the state or country in an address.**

Post-Test

1. In the first blank space next to each adjective below, write the form of the adjective that compares two things. In the second blank, write the form that compares more than two things.

   a. hearty _____ _____

   b. intelligent _____ _____

   c. smooth _____ _____

2. Compare a bicycle and an automobile. On the following lines, list two ways they are similar and two ways they are different.

   Similar: _____

   _____

   Different: _____

   _____

3. Write S next to each simile below. Write M next to each metaphor.

   a. _____ The traffic was a river rushing through the city.

   b. _____ Tim's clothes were as rumpled as his unmade bed.

   c. _____ The bull roared through the field like a hurricane.

4. Underline the more specific adjective in each sentence.

   a. Most of the fifth-graders said the play was (bad, uninteresting).

   b. However, they thought the stage scenery was (colorful, neat).

   c. Some (good, experienced) actors would improve the play.

5. Choose one of the pairs of items below. Then write a paragraph that tells how the two items are alike. Next, write a second paragraph that tells how they differ.

   a horse and a camel   a radio and a TV   a school and a house

48

unit **4**
Writing Details

Things to Remember About Writing with Details

Details are small bits of information.

Writing Tips
- Use details to help you write a good description.
- Choose details that fit your purpose in writing.
- Use as many of your senses as you can when writing descriptions.
- Describe characters by telling what they look like, what their character traits are, and how they act in certain situations.

Revising Tips
- Use adverbs and adverbial phrases to describe *how*, *when*, or *where*.

Proofreading Tips Check to see that you have
- used quotation marks around a direct quotation
- set off a quotation from the rest of the sentence with a comma, question mark, or exclamation point
- capitalized the first word of a quotation

1 Writing descriptions

Have you ever heard anyone say, "It's hard to describe—you should have seen it"? If you were to meet one of the creatures pictured here, you would probably find it hard to describe. But you *can* write a good description if you use details.

A. Read each description below. Then, under the picture, write the name of the creature that fits the description.

The leucocrotta is about the size of a zebra. It has the neck, chest, and tail of a lion. Its head, which looks like a badger's head, has a smile that reaches from ear to ear. The leucocrotta has the legs and hooves of a deer, and it is very fast.

The manticore has the head and face of a human, except that it has three rows of teeth. Its body is strong and shaped like a lion's. The manticore's tail is long and thin, and it has a stinger on the end.

B. The first animal pictured above is a chimera. Label it. Then write its description on the following lines.

_____

_____

_____

_____

C. Sometimes very simple objects, things you see every day, are the most difficult to describe. Look at these objects. Write descriptions of two of them on the lines that follow. Include as many details as you can that describe the size, shape, material, and uses of each object.

 Riddles can be detailed descriptions of objects. However, the details are usually incomplete or given in a way that is meant to confuse or mystify. Here is a riddle that describes something you probably use every day. Perhaps you have one in your hand right now.

My hard round body grows shorter; my pink tail will disappear; yet, still, I leave my winding trail.*

Think of two or three everyday objects to write riddles about. First, decide what details you will mention. Then think about how you will present these details. Write your riddles on a separate sheet of paper.

*Did you guess that it's a pencil?

You can write a good description if you use details.

2 Focusing on details

In a way, writing is like taking a picture. If you do not take time to focus the camera, the picture will be fuzzy. In order to describe an object well, you must look at it carefully. The longer you look at something, the more details you will notice.

A. Look at these pictures. The one on the left is out of focus. But the one on the right is clear. On the lines that follow, list at least five details about the house in the clear picture.

_____

_____

_____

_____

_____

B. Step inside the house for a moment. This is the living room. Write a paragraph that tells what you see in this room. The topic sentence is provided for you. Use details to develop the topic sentence.

Walking into the living room was like stepping into another time.

_____

_____

_____

_____

_____

 When a photographer aims a camera, certain objects to the left or right of the camera are left out of the picture. Similarly, a writer uses some details and leaves out others. The details included often depend on the purpose.

Pretend you are one of the following people. Look for or make up details that suit your purpose about the house pictured on these pages. Then write about the house on a separate sheet of paper.

a real estate agent who is writing an ad in order to sell the house

a writer who is describing the house as the setting for a ghost story

a neighbor writing a letter asking the city to tear down the house and build a park

Good writing focuses carefully on details. Often, the details you describe depend on your purpose.

53

3 Appealing to the senses

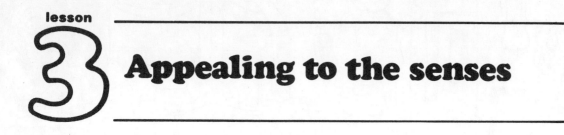

A photographer can appeal to only one sense—sight. A good writer, however, through imagination, appeals to all the senses—**sight, hearing, smell, taste,** and **touch.**

A. Imagine that you are alone in the basement of an old house. The batteries of your flashlight have just gone dead. It is so dark that you cannot even see your own hand in front of your face. You must *feel* your way, step by step, through the dark basement, up the stairs, and out. What do you touch? Does anything brush against you? On the lines that follow, describe in detail four things that you feel as you try to get out of the house.

_____

_____

_____

_____

_____

B. As you walk through the house you begin to hear sounds. Is it the wind or an insect—or maybe a ghost? Use your imagination to describe what you might hear in an empty house. Describe four sounds and tell where they come from.

_____

_____

_____

_____

_____

C. Eventually you reach a door and escape outside. What sounds do you hear now? List five sounds you might hear outside the empty house.

_____

_____

_____

_____

D. After your adventure in the house, you are frightened and tired. Most of all you are hungry. You head right for home and raid the refrigerator. On the lines that follow, tell what you ate and how it tasted.

_____

_____

_____

_____

Write On

The sense of smell is the hardest sense to write about. Many people are not very aware of smells. Also, there aren't too many words to describe smells. Yet smell can change your mood—it can bring back memories, make you think of spring, or make you hungry.

Take a walk in your imagination through your house or neighborhood. What smells do you remember? How would you describe them? On another sheet of paper, write a list of at least ten things your nose remembers. Then describe them in a paragraph.

_____

Use as many of your senses as you can when writing descriptions.

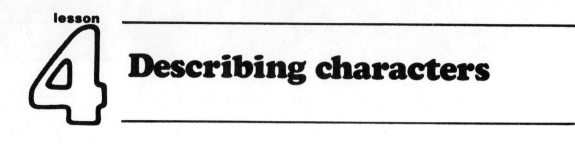

Describing characters

A. Read this description of Ichabod Crane. Then put a check mark under the picture that fits the description.

He was tall but exceedingly lank, with narrow shoulders, long arms and legs, hands that dangled a mile out of his sleeves, feet that might have served for shovels, and his whole frame hung together most loosely. His head was small and flat at top, with huge ears, large green glassy eyes, and a long snipe nose, so that it looked like a weathercock perched upon his spindle neck. . . .

—*Washington Irving*

B. Try using words to paint a picture of a character's face and body. You can describe a real person or make up a person. You can be funny or be true to life. Use the following list to record important details.

Face: _____

Hair: _____

Size: _____

Clothes: _____

56

Gestures and Movements: _____

_____

In addition to describing physical appearance, writers use details to tell what a person is like. Small details are clues—they show **character traits.** They tell whether a person is brave, nervous, intelligent, proud, and/or cruel. Read this sentence about Emma Woodhouse and see what you learn about her.

Emma Woodhouse, handsome, clever, and rich, with a comfortable home and happy disposition, seemed to unite some of the best blessings of existence; and had lived nearly twenty-one years in the world with very little to distress or vex her.

—Jane Austen

C. List two details about Emma's character.

_____

_____

D. On the following lines, tell about two traits of the character you described in part **B.**

_____

_____

_____

_____

_____

 Characters come alive when we see them in a situation where they speak, act, think, and feel. Use details in a paragraph to show how your character from part **B** will react in one of the following situations.

a plane with engine trouble   the Olympics
a blackout   a train where a murder has
a close basketball game   been committed

When you describe characters, tell what they look like, their character traits, and how they act in certain situations.

5 Using dialogue

Writers often present the exact words that characters speak. These words are called **dialogue.** Dialogue helps us to learn more about the characters and the situation. Read this dialogue between Mrs. Trumble, Asa's mother, and Ms. Gomez, Asa's teacher.

"Asa's always been a good boy," Mrs. Trumble said softly.

Ms. Gomez frowned before she spoke. "I've been disturbed by Asa's behavior this week. He had fifteen white mice in my classroom on Monday. It made spelling impossible."

"Well, scientists often use white mice—"

"Not during spelling tests, Mrs. Trumble." The teacher's dark eyes flashed. "The rocket explosion in the gym this morning, however, was the last straw."

A. Think about what you've learned about the characters. Then continue the conversation on the lines below. Have each speaker say at least one more sentence. Check your punctuation with the rules on page 62.

_____

_____

_____

_____

_____

Dialogue should sound natural. It should sound the way people speak. A person's speech depends on many things—age, education, occupation, birthplace, and situation.

B. On the lines that follow, rewrite the following dialogue so that it would sound natural for two-fifth graders in your school.

"Pardon me, Jane, are you engaged this evening? If you're free, perhaps we might attend the cinema."

"What a splendid proposition, Harriet. Let me glance through my engagement book. No, I haven't any prior commitments."

"Excellent! I shall make inquiries as to the exact hour of the showing."

_____

_____

_____

_____

_____

_____

_____

_____

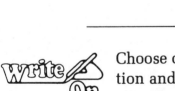

Choose one of the following situations. Use dialogue to develop the situation and the characters. Or, if you prefer, you may make up your own situation. Write your dialogue on a separate sheet of paper.

1. A discussion between two pigeons about which park in town is best for bread crumbs.
2. A telephone conversation between a parent and child who have not seen each other for two years.
3. A conversation between you and the character you described on pages 56 and 57 (parts **B** and **D**).

Dialogue is the exact words characters speak. You use dialogue to reveal more about the characters and the situation. Dialogue should sound natural.

Revising

6 Writing with adverbs

Adverbs tell how, when, or where something happens.

Gino is singing <u>loudly</u> <u>in the shower</u> <u>now</u>.

An adverb can be a single word, such as *loudly* or *now*. Many adverbs are formed from adjectives by adding *ly*:

loud loud<u>ly</u>   fond fond<u>ly</u>   slow slow<u>ly</u>

A **phrase,** or group of words, can also act like an adverb. These **adverbial phrases** begin with **prepositions.** For example, the adverbial phrase *in the shower* begins with the preposition *in.* Here are some other adverbial phrases:

He left <u>at midnight</u>.   She hid <u>under the bed</u>.   I walked <u>with speed</u>.

A. Complete the following sentences by writing an adverb or an adverbial phrase which answers the question in parentheses.

1. I said I'd go trick or treating _____.
   (when?)

2. That jack-o'-lantern is sitting _____.
   (where?)

3. I don't like the way it grins so _____.
   (how?)

4. I see green gauze ghosts _____.
   (where?)

5. I don't mind skeletons at all; they usually act _____.
   (how?)

6. It's odd that there weren't any goblins _____.
   (when?)

You can use adverbs to answer more than one question in a sentence. For example:

Joanna was swimming. (Where and when was she swimming?)
Joanna was swimming underwater at three o'clock.

You can also vary the position of the adverbs in a sentence. For example:

At three o'clock, Joanna was swimming underwater.

B. Rewrite each of the following sentences on the lines below. Add an adverb that answers the question in parentheses.

1. Oscar plays the trombone. (How and where does he play it?)

_____

_____

2. Mr. Lopez found the box. (Where and when did he find it?)

_____

_____

3. The ghost has disappeared! (How and when did it disappear?)

_____

_____

Writers sometimes use **dialogue tags** to tell exactly how something is said. These tags often consist of a verb and an adverb.

"That's the last drop of water," the soldier muttered grimly.

C. Complete these sentences by writing a dialogue tag with a verb and an adverb. Make your words express the idea in parentheses.

1. "I never promised you the moon," Mr. Krinsky _____

_____. (anger)

2. "What do you mean you lost my car?" Mrs. Dinsmere _____

_____. (confusion)

Look over the "Write On" paragraphs you've written for this unit. Choose one to improve with adverbs or adverbial phrases. Rewrite your paragraph on a separate sheet of paper.

_____

Use adverbs and adverbial phrases to tell how, when, and where.

Proofreading

lesson 7 — Writing quotations correctly

"Did you go to the Halloween party last night?" asked Gil.
"Yes, Gil, I came as a radio!" replied Jill.

This conversation is written as a dialogue. The spoken words are set off at the beginning and end by **quotation marks.** Quotation marks show that the words are exactly what the speaker said. We call these words a **direct quotation.**

In dialogue, every speaker begins in a new paragraph. This makes it easy to keep track of different speakers.

Gil said, "Who else was there?"
"Just about everybody. It was great. The best part was when Alfie got his head stuck in a pumpkin."

When you write dialogue, you don't always have to repeat the name of the speaker. Since each new speech begins as a new paragraph, you can tell in the dialogue above that the second line is said by Jill, the other speaker.

Look over the punctuation in the two sections of dialogue above. It follows these rules:

1. **The first word in a quotation is capitalized.**
2. **The words within a quotation can end in a comma, question mark, or exclamation point. They never end in a period unless it marks the end of the whole sentence, as in the last line of the dialogue** (after *pumpkin*).

62

3. Notice that when the speaker's name comes before the quotation, you add a comma before the quotation marks. (In the example above, the comma comes after *Gil said.*)

A. Read these sentences carefully. Add the missing punctuation in each one. Use the rules to help you.

1. Where were you at 12:30 on the morning of the twenty-third asked the lawyer.

2. I was in the kitchen said the witness.

3. And what were you doing there he cried.

4. I was making a . . . a . . . chicken sandwich she stammered.

5. Exactly what did you put in your chicken sandwich, Mrs. Kelp asked the lawyer, with a triumphant gleam in his eye.

6. The witness licked her lips nervously and whispered Watercress, salt, and butter.

B. On the lines below, write a conversation you've had recently with a friend or relative. Use correct punctuation marks to indicate a direct quotation.

_____

_____

_____

_____

_____

_____

_____

When you proofread your writing, check to see that:
- **you use quotation marks around a direct quotation**
- **you set off a quotation from the rest of the sentence with a comma, question mark, or exclamation point**
- **you capitalize the first word of a quotation**

Post-Test

1. Write the letter of the picture described below.

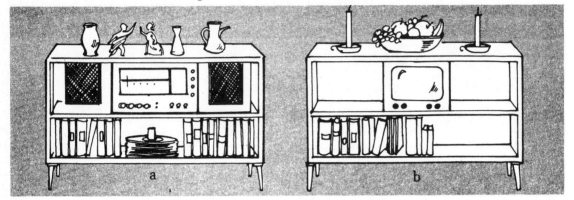

_____ The cabinet had three shelves. The bottom shelf was filled with books and records. The middle shelf held a stereo and speakers, while a few delicate vases and statues were arranged on the top shelf.

2. Write which of the five senses each description most appeals to.

   a. Fran ran her hand along the cold, smooth stones. _____

   b. Kira bit into the apple's sweet juiciness. _____

3. Add an adverb or adverbial phrase to each sentence below.

   a. The huge mirror crashed (where) _____.

   b. The elephants will charge (when) _____.

   c. Jim's mule danced (how) _____.

4. Add the punctuation that is missing in this dialogue.

   A man took a sip of coffee. Yucch! he said. This coffee tastes like mud.

   It should said the waitress. It was ground this morning.

5. Choose one of the following items and describe it in a paragraph. Include as many details as you can in the paragraph.

   a pizza   roller skates   a flashlight   a hammer

unit 5
Writing Facts and Opinions

Things to Remember About Writing Facts and Opinions

A **fact** is something that can be tested or checked. An **opinion** is what someone thinks or feels.

Writing

- Base your opinions on facts to make them more convincing.
- Use facts that explain *who, what, when, where,* and *why* in news stories. Put opinions in quotations when writing news stories.

Revising

- Combine short, choppy sentences into longer, smoother sentences.
- Use *and* to combine subjects, predicates, adjectives, or adverbs.

Proofreading

Check to see that you have

- used the plain form of present-tense verbs with plural subjects or the pronouns *I* and *you*
- used the *s* form of present-tense verbs with singular subjects other than *I* and *you*
- used the plain form of present-tense verbs when the subject is two nouns joined by *and*

1 Writing sentences of fact and opinion

It is important to be able to tell the difference between facts and opinions. A **fact** is a statement that can be tested or checked to see if it is true. An **opinion** expresses someone's feelings or thoughts. An opinion cannot be tested or checked. Some words—such as *think, believe, like, hate, best,* and *worst* — are clues that a statement is an opinion.

A. Jane and Shana went to the Ritz Theater. Both girls did not like the theater. Read what they wrote, and answer the questions below.

Jane
The Ritz is a horrible place. It is so awful that I hate it. You can't imagine how unpleasant it is there. The seats are really bad, and so is the movie screen. Even the soda and popcorn taste terrible.

Shana
The Ritz Theater was built in 1933, and the owners haven't made any repairs since then. Over half of the seats are broken. There are nine large holes in the movie screen. Last Saturday, twelve patrons complained about warm soda and stale popcorn.

1. Which writer has used facts? _____

2. Which writer has written only opinions? _____

3. Draw a line under each opinion clue word.

B. Facts and opinions are often contained in the same piece of writing. Read this ad. Look for statements that you can check. Look for opinion clue words.

> Tonight come down to the Ritz, Bogville's finest movie theater. The Ritz, located at 52 Bogview Road, has a new show every week. This week see the exciting hit *Under the Weather.* Showings are at 8:00 and 10:00 P.M. Relax in our delightfully air-cooled theater. Sink into our comfortable seats.

1. Write three facts found in the ad. Use complete sentences.

_____

_____

_____

2. Write three opinions found in the ad. Use complete sentences.

_____

_____

_____

C. People sometimes use facts to form opinions. Read these facts about the lunches at Bogview School.

1. Of the food that is served, 63 percent is not eaten.
2. The meat loaf contains less than 6 percent meat.
3. The cook serves chicken croquettes every Wednesday; nine out of ten students refuse to eat the croquettes.

Write one opinion about Bogview lunches based on the facts above.

_____

_____

 If your opinions are based on facts, they will be more convincing. Choose one of the opinions below, or make up an opinion of your own. On another paper, write a short paragraph using the opinion you chose as the topic. Give at least three facts to support your opinion.

Parks are important to people.
Pollution is very dangerous.
Automobiles are great.
Automobiles are trouble.

Facts can be tested or checked; opinions cannot be. Opinions give someone's thoughts or feelings. Opinions based on facts are more convincing.

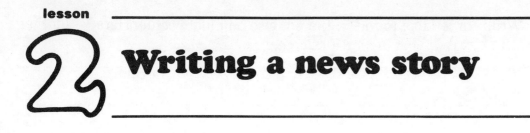

Writing a news story

A news story contains facts. The facts in a news story usually answer the questions *who, what, when, where,* and sometimes *why.* We call these the **wh questions.** Read this news story.

Farmer Sees UFO

Barnsville, October 9—Thaddeus Koslowitz of Meadow Farm reported seeing an unidentified flying object in his north field last night around midnight. He described the UFO as a round, bright object that hovered about seven meters off the ground, played music for about five minutes, and then sped off to the west.

"It was really a strange sight. I wasn't exactly scared—just surprised," Koslowitz stated.

A. On the lines below, fill in the facts from the news story above.

Who: _____

What: _____

When: _____

Where: _____

Newspaper reporters state only the facts of a story. A reporter may state an opinion or feeling if it is a quotation. **Quotations** are the exact words spoken by people.

B. Are there any opinions given in the story above? List them, and underline any opinion clue words.

_____

_____

C. **Headlines** state the main idea of a story in a few words. Here is another headline from the October 9 Barnsville paper.

Barnsville Disc Jockey Plays Music From Blimp

Does this headline give you an idea for the *why* of the story on page 68? If so, fill in the reason below.

Why: _____

_____

The first paragraph of a news story is called the **lead.** The lead gives the important facts of a story. The lead should also be interesting and well written, so that a reader will continue to read the news story.

D. Write a lead paragraph for the headline below. Make up specific facts that explain *who, what, when, where,* and *why.*

Barnsville Disc Jockey Plays Music From Blimp

_____

_____

_____

_____

_____

_____

 On another sheet of paper, write a news story based on one of the headlines below or on a headline you make up. Use a good, factual lead paragraph that answers the *wh* questions. Try to include a quotation or two that states an opinion.

New Museum to Open
Woman Finds Strange Footprints
Invention Changes People's Lives

_____

News stories contain facts that explain <u>who</u>, <u>what</u>, <u>when</u>, <u>where</u>, and sometimes <u>why</u>. Opinions in news stories should only be found in quotations.

Writing in a diary

A **journal** or **diary** is a book in which a person keeps a record of what happens in his or her life. People write both facts and opinions in their journals or diaries. The words *journal* and *diary* once meant "daily." People often write in them every day.

Here is one day's entry from the journal of Sargeant John Ordway. He traveled with Lewis and Clark on their famous expedition. For the most part, Ordway listed facts in his journal.

> Thursday, June 28, 1804. Pleasant. I went out hunting two and a half miles and passed a fine spring running from under the hills. I drank hearty of the water and found it the best and coolest I have seen in the country. . . . One man saw several buffelow up the Kansas River. This is 366 miles from the mouth of Missouris. The latitude is 38° 31^m 13^s North. The width of the Missouris here is 500 yards wide.

A.   Think about the last seven days. What have you been doing? Choose one of these days. Where were you? What did you do? Write a journal entry which tells four facts about that day. Be sure to begin by writing the day and date.

_____

_____

_____

_____

_____

_____

Diaries or journals are places to write down opinions and feelings. Writing them down is one way to get them off your mind. Read part of a fourteen-year-old's diary on the next page.

70

> Oh! that awful Catherine. Acting so dramatic and la-dee-da, just because she got the part in the play. I saw her bat her big eyes at Mr. Fiore and say, "I'll do everything in my power to make the play a grand success." Her power! Who does she think she is—Catherine the Great? Katharine Hepburn? The only reason I didn't get the part was because I wasn't tall enough.

B. On the lines below, write your opinions about something that has been on your mind lately. Choose something that you have strong feelings about.

_____

_____

_____

_____

_____

_____

Write On

Pretend you're a historian who finds one of the following journals.

> a journal kept by Columbus when he was sailing on the Santa Maria
> the journal Washington wrote in at Valley Forge
> a diary kept by a runaway slave in the early 1800s

Or, if you prefer, you may "find" the diary of some other person who played a role in history. What might the journal reveal? Use your imagination to write an entry from one of these journals on a separate sheet of paper.

A journal or diary is a record a person keeps that can contain both facts and opinions. Many people write in their journals or diaries daily.

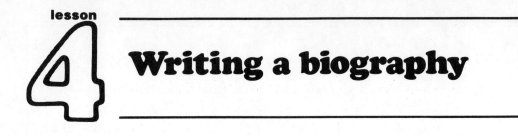

Writing a biography

A **biography** is the story of a person's life. A biography contains important facts about the person. It may also contain opinions and conclusions based on these facts. A **biographer** is a person who writes a biography.

A. If you were a biographer, what person would you write about? Think about someone you know and respect. You might choose a person in your family, a neighbor, or a friend. Choose anyone you know about—except yourself. Try to give brief answers to the following questions.

1. Where and when was the person born? _____

_____

2. What were the person's family and home like? _____

_____

3. Where did the person go to school? _____

_____

4. What jobs has the person had? _____

_____

5. What special hobbies, sports, or crafts does the person enjoy?

_____

_____

6. What interesting things have happened to the person? _____

_____

_____

_____

B. Biographers often use facts to form opinions and conclusions about a person. You have just written about someone you respect. Think about why you admire this person. Is the person good, honest, intelligent, kind? On the lines below, write several sentences that tell your opinions about this person. Try to include some facts and details that make your opinions more convincing.

_____

_____

_____

_____

_____

_____

This is a Blue-Nosed Widge. You probably haven't seen one around lately. Write a short biography of this widge, the kind that might appear in an encyclopedia. Give the following information: Where was the widge born? What kind of family does the widge have? What special things has this widge done? Why don't we see many widges anymore?

_____

A biography contains important facts about a person's life. Biographers often use facts to form opinions and conclusions about the person.

5 Writing a myth

Have you ever wondered why things are the way they are? Why is grass green or the sky blue? Why are there rainbows? One way to explain things that you don't understand is to make up a myth. A **myth** explains something by telling a story. Read the two explanations of rainbows below.

A

Long ago there were many gods. They lived far away in Asgard. The gods often traveled down to Midgard, where people lived.

"If we built a bridge, the trip to Midgard would be shorter," said Frey. He was the god of rain and sunshine.

"Yes," agreed his sister, Freya. She was the goddess of beauty. "But with what will we build the bridge?"

"Fire and air and water," replied Frey.

And so they built the beautiful rainbow bridge. And you can see it in times of rain and sunshine when they travel. You can even see the red fire and the blue air and the green water that they built it with.

B

A rainbow appears when the sun shines through water droplets in the air. As a ray of sunshine enters and leaves a water droplet, it is bent, or refracted. This bending lets us see the many colors that make up a ray of white sunlight. In order for you to see a rainbow, the sun, the center of the rainbow, and your eye must be on the same line. If the sun is high in the sky, a rainbow will not appear.

A. Answer these questions about the two explanations on page 74.

1. Which one contains facts, *A* or *B*? _____

2. List three facts contained in this explanation.

_____

_____

_____

3. A myth is a story. Letter _____ is a myth.

4. How is the myth different from the other explanation?

_____

_____

B. Write a short myth. In a few sentences, explain one of the following.

Why does a skunk have a white stripe?
Why are lemons sour?
Where does snow come from?

_____

_____

_____

_____

_____

_____

Write On — What have you often wondered about? Think of a question for which you don't know the answer. Then, on a separate sheet of paper, make up a myth to explain the answer to your question.

_____

A myth is a story made up to explain something that is not understood.

Revising

6 Combining sentences

There are many ways to combine sentences. The ideas contained in some short, choppy sentences can be combined into one sentence with the word *and.* Look at these examples.

Combining Subjects: Ned collects snakes. Madge collects snakes.
> Ned <u>and</u> Madge collect snakes.

Combining Verbs or Predicates: Lori bought the coat. Lori paid for it.
> Lori bought the coat <u>and</u> paid for it.

Combining Adjectives: The day was sunny. The day was warm.
> The day was sunny <u>and</u> warm.

Combining Adverbs: John eats quickly. John eats noisily.
> John eats quickly <u>and</u> noisily.

A. Combine each pair of sentences below into one sentence. Use the examples above to help you.

1. The bus was crowded. The bus was dirty.

   _____

2. The mountains were blue. The sky was blue.

   _____

3. The river flows restlessly. The river flows rapidly.

   _____

4. Mirra opened one eye. Mirra yawned.

   _____

5. Leslie ran to the door. Leslie opened it.

   _____

   Adjectives usually have one of two positions in a sentence: before a noun or after a form of *be,* such as *is* or *were.* A way to combine short, choppy sentences that contain adjectives is to move the adjective to a position in front of a noun.

Look at these examples.

The car was yellow. It was a convertible.
The car was a yellow convertible.

The cat was scrawny. It was hungry.
The scrawny cat was hungry.

B. Combine each pair of sentences below. Use the examples above to help you.

1. That dress is pink. It is attractive.

_____

2. That boy is tall. He plays basketball.

_____

3. My sweater is brand new. It is already dirty.

_____

C. The paragraph below has several short, choppy sentences. Rewrite the paragraph on the lines that follow. Combine sentences to make the paragraph smoother.

The woman sighed. She shuffled her feet. She looked at the clock on the wall. The clock was huge. The woman was impatient. She was nervous. Suddenly she heard a noise behind her. It was soft. She jumped up. She ran to the door.

_____

_____

_____

_____

 Look back at the "Write On" exercises you've written in this unit. Do any have short, choppy sentences? Choose one paragraph to rewrite. Combine sentences where you can to make your paragraph smoother.

_____

You can sometimes combine two short, choppy sentences into one longer, smoother sentence.

_____

77

Proofreading

lesson 7

Making subjects and verbs agree

Every sentence has a subject and a verb. Present-tense verbs have two forms: the **plain form,** like *play,* and the **s form,** like *plays.* The verb form must go with, or **agree** with, the subject. Look at these examples.

Gloria plays softball.　　　　The girls play softball.
She plays softball.　　　　　I play softball.
Gloria and Juan play softball.　You play softball.
They play softball.　　　　　We play softball.

A. Use the sentences above to help you complete the following generalizations.

1. When the subject is a singular noun or the pronoun *it, she,* or *he,* use the

    _____ form of the verb.

2. When the subject is a plural noun, two nouns joined by *and,* or the pro-

    noun *I, you, we,* or *they,* use the _____ form of the verb.

   To make the s form of most verbs, you add *s* or *es.* Some verbs change form slightly.

do do<u>es</u>   bury bur<u>ies</u>   have h<u>as</u>

B. Underline the correct form of the present-tense verb in the following sentences.

1. Every day I (jog, jogs) along the river.
2. My sister (run, runs) five miles before school.
3. She (go, goes) around the park five times.
4. My two spaniels (scurry, scurries) next to me most of the way.
5. Then they (take, takes) off after a cat or a bicycle.
6. Two police officers always (pass, passes) us.
7. They (smile, smiles) and (wave, waves) at us.

78

The word *be* has some special present-tense forms:

I <u>am</u> singing.　　You <u>are</u> singing.　　He <u>is</u> singing.
We <u>are</u> singing.　　The girls <u>are</u> singing.　　They <u>are</u> singing.

C.　Fill in the blank with the correct present-tense form of *be*.

1. I _____ going to the movies tonight.

2. Tom _____ coming with me.

3. We _____ taking the bus downtown.

4. Philip and Chris _____ meeting us there.

5. Terry, you _____ welcome to come too.

D.　Write a short diary entry for your favorite TV or book character. Tell what you think she or he might be doing or thinking now. Use present-tense verb forms. Underline each verb form you use.

_____

_____

_____

_____

_____

When you proofread your writing, check to see that any present-tense verbs you use agree with the subject.

Post-Test

1. Write *F* after each sentence that is a fact. Write *O* after each opinion.

   a. The egg has a brown shell. _____

   b. The yolk looks pale and funny. _____

   c. The carton says it is Grade A. _____

   d. It will taste better scrambled with milk. _____

2. Read these facts about a writer. Then write an opinion based on the facts.

   a. Robert Jones's lastest novel has sold a million copies.
   b. His short stories have appeared in fifty different magazines.
   c. Four movies have been based on books by Jones.

   _____

3. Combine each pair of sentences below.
   a. One cup was broken. Two plates were broken.

   _____

   b. The rains poured down. The rains washed away our tent.

   _____

   c. The alligator is hungry. It is next to your legs.

   _____

4. In each sentence below, underline the correct form of the verb.
   a. Ella (play, plays) the banjo up on the roof.
   b. Junior and Flip (hurry, hurries) up to hear her.
   c. I (like, likes) the music too.
   d. The whole neighborhood (hear, hears) it.

5. Write a paragraph on one of the topics below. First write an opinion about the topic. Then write at least three facts that support your opinion.

   City Life   Suburban Life   Country Life
   Friends   Pets   Space Exploration

unit 6
Writing About Cause and Effect

Things to Remember When Writing About Cause and Effect

A **cause** tells why something happens. An **effect** is what happens.

 Writing Tips
- Use a series of cause sentences and effect sentences when telling what happened in a story.
- Use words and word groups like *because, since, as a result of,* and *therefore* to join cause sentences with effect sentences.
- Use details that help the reader guess the cause when writing a mystery.

 Revising Tips
- Use conjunctions and subordinate conjunctions to combine short, choppy sentences into smoother sentences.

 Proofreading Tips
Check to see that you have
- used the correct past-tense forms
- used the correct verb forms after *have* or *has*

1 Writing cause and effect sentences

When something happens, we often ask "Why?" When we ask why, we are looking for a cause. A **cause** tells why something happens. An **effect** is what happens.

A. Riddles often ask why. Read each riddle on the left below. Then find its correct cause. Write the number of the riddle next to the cause which explains it.

1. Why does the ocean roar all night?

2. Why are Clem's slacks always wet?

3. Why does Clem sleep on the chandelier?

4. Why do spiders spin webs?

a. _____ The labels say "Wash and Wear."

b. _____ They don't know how to knit.

c. _____ You'd roar too if your bed was filled with sand.

d. _____ He's a light sleeper.

Look at each picture below. Picture *A* shows several causes. Picture *B* shows the effects of these causes.

A   B

B. On the following lines, write two pairs of sentences about the pictures. In the first sentence, state the cause. In the second sentence, state the effect. One has been done to get you started.

1. *The girl is running with a kite. The kite is flying high.*

2. _____

   _____

3. _____

   _____

C. The same things happen to Clem Cloudhead every day. But poor Clem doesn't know why. Write a sentence that tells Clem why each thing might happen.

1. Clem always wakes up late. _____

   _____

2. Whenever Clem fries eggs, they burn. _____

   _____

3. By the time Clem gets to the bus stop, the school bus is always gone. ____

   _____

4. Clem always spells the words on the spelling test wrong. _____

   _____

Write On

Choose one of the sentences below or think up your own. Then, on a separate sheet of paper, write a short story. Use a series of cause-and-effect sentences to tell what happened.

   I planted magic beanstalk beans in my windowbox.
   I forgot to set my alarm the night before the big game.
   I was caught in a bad windstorm.

In cause-and-effect writing, one sentence gives the cause, or reason, and the other sentence tells the effect, or what happened.

2 Writing with cause and effect words and phrases

Certain words and phrases are clues that a cause or effect is being stated. Some common cause-and-effect clue words and phrases are *because, since, as a result of, due to, therefore,* and *consequently.*

A. Read the following sentences. Draw a line under the cause-and-effect clue in each sentence. Then draw a circle around the cause part of the sentence.

1. "Daughter," the father said, "I know you really want to be a truckdriver when you grow up, and therefore I'll never stand in your way."

2. You probably haven't heard the joke about the bed since it hasn't been made up yet.

3. *Smiles* is the longest word in the dictionary because there is a mile between its first and last letter.

4. Every player insists on raising a racket; consequently, tennis is the noisiest sport.

5. Due to the very cold temperature of the lake water, Clem went swimming in his sweater.

B. Combine each pair of sentences below to form one sentence. Use the cause-and-effect word in parentheses.

1. The restaurant was on the moon. It had very little atmosphere. (since)

_____

_____

2. Johnny told his mother he didn't want to write clearly. The teacher would know he couldn't spell. (because)

_____

_____

3. The rooster couldn't figure out where the sun went at night. He stayed up until it finally dawned on him. (therefore)

_____

_____

C. Add a cause-and-effect word or phrase and a conclusion to each humorous sentence below. Your conclusion can be either the cause or the effect of the stated sentence.

1. I forgot to tell Dad about the escaped tiger hiding in the garage.

_____

_____

2. I forgot I was filling the bathtub and went to Diane's to watch TV.

_____

_____

3. There are a large number of alligators in the town swimming pool.

_____

_____

On a separate sheet of paper, write a joke or a humorous story that contains cause-and-effect words and phrases. Underline each clue you use. You might want to start your story this way.

"Waiter! There's a fly in my soup," the angry diner shouted.

_____

Words and phrases like <u>since</u>, <u>because</u>, and <u>as a result</u> are often clues that a cause or effect is being stated.

3 Writing a science explanation

Both Mug and Zug give causes for the eclipse. But which caveman gives a cause that can be proven? Scientists look for causes that can be seen and understood.

A. Read how Mug explains certain things which happen. Then tell how a scientist might explain them. Write the cause for each effect on the lines below.

1. Falling snow

    Mug's Cause: Giant ice swans fly high above and drop their white feathers.

    Scientific Cause: _____

    _____

2. Thunder

    Mug's Cause: The clouds fight with the sun.

    Scientific Cause: _____

    _____

86

B. Mug has just found a bicycle in his cave. He isn't quite sure how to use it. Explain it to Mug as you complete each sentence by writing an effect.

1. By turning the handlebars, Mug, you can _____

_____

2. Pushing up and down on the pedals with your feet will _____

_____

3. If you grasp the handbrakes tightly, _____

_____

Scientists can predict the effect of a cause. They have learned from previous experience or experimentation what to expect. When the weather forecaster sees clouds in the sky, he can predict rain.

C. Tell how Zug would complete the following sentences, using scientific predictions.

1. Since the temperature has dropped below freezing, Zug predicts that

   the rain will _____.

2. In the fall, Zug predicts that the leaves will soon _____.

3. If Zug puts a twig in the fire, he can predict that the twig will _____.

4. If Zug drops a stone in the lake, Zug can predict that the stone will

   _____.

 Think of an effect that you saw recently. Perhaps you saw a machine pumping gasoline, or water turning into ice in a freezer. How would a scientist explain the effect? How might Mug explain the same effect? Write the two explanations on a separate paper. You may use an encyclopedia or a science book for your scientific explanation.

In a scientific explanation, the cause of an effect can be understood. Scientists also can predict the effect of a cause.

---

4 Writing about a mystery

A **mystery** is an effect with an unknown cause. You can solve a mystery by finding a cause which explains it. Mystery writers need imagination to dream up causes that puzzle their readers. Look at the picture below.

A. Use your imagination to make up a mystery. Find two things happening in the picture. First, write the effect that you observe—in other words, tell what is going on. Next, write a probable cause of the effect. Last, use your imagination to make up a "mysterious" cause. Follow this example.

> Effect: A woman digs a hole in her yard.
> Probable Cause: She wants to plant flowers or vegetables.
> Mysterious Cause: She must bury a fortune in stolen gold.

1. Effect: _____

   Probable Cause: _____

   Mysterious Cause: _____

2. Effect: _____

Probable Cause: _____

Mysterious Cause: _____

B. Clues are an important part of a mystery. Clues are usually details that help us guess the cause of a mystery. Read these descriptions.

The man rounded the corner and smiled at the women. He ran all the way to Third and Maple, where he dropped something into the gutter. Then his friend picked him up in a car.

The running man tried to slow down when he saw the women. He gave them a forced smile, but he kept looking over his shoulder nervously. His hand never left a package stuffed inside his jacket. He seemed to hide his face with his hand when a police car passed. He threw a heavy metal object into the storm drain at Third and Maple. Then a big black car with out-of-state plates roared up. The man jumped in and shouted orders to the driver.

1. List four details the second writer gives that the first does not.

_____

_____

_____

_____

2. Tell what you think is causing the man to act as he does.

_____

_____

Choose one of your ideas from part **A** or **B** to use as the basis of a short mystery story. On another piece of paper, write your mystery and solution. Use details as clues.

A mystery is an effect with an unknown cause. In a mystery story, details are often provided as clues to the solution.

Writing a story problem and solution

There's an old tale about a woman with a stubborn pig. The pig refused to climb over the steps of a fence. The woman couldn't go home without the pig, and the pig wouldn't budge. The woman got angry and asked a dog to bite the pig and chase it over the fence. The dog said, "No." That made her more angry, so she asked a stick to beat the dog, but the stick refused. Next, she asked a fire to burn the stick. "No," the fire replied.

The poor woman kept being refused. Some water refused to quench the fire. An ox refused to drink the water. A rope refused to choke the ox. A rat refused to gnaw the rope.

Finally, she asked a cat to catch the rat, and the cat agreed. A **chain reaction** of causes and effects began. The cat tried to get the rat, but before it could, the rat started to gnaw on the rope. Almost immediately the rope started to choke the ox, but the ox . . .

A. Tell what happens next. Write a chain of cause-and-effect sentences. Tell how the woman's problem is finally solved.

1. _____

2. _____

3. _____

4. _____

5. _____

6. _____

7. _____

In many stories, a character has a problem—like the woman who wanted to get home. A series of events occur. Often one thing leads to another—like the chain of causes and effects you completed in part **A**. Finally, the problem is solved.

B. Try to develop a story in which one thing leads to another. Use cause-and-effect sentences whenever possible. You may use one or more of these characters in your story, or you may make up your own characters.

> Rachel Goldstein: a young girl with a photographic memory
> Ranger: a brilliant German shepherd
> Mr. Alonzo: a wise old man that no one listens to

You may use one or two of these objects, or **props,** in your story, or you may make up your own:

a missing mailbox	an antique sword	a bag filled with diamonds
a UFO	an old-fashioned car	a hidden cabin
a fire truck	a tall elm tree	a train that never stops

On the lines below, write your story problem. Then write a chain of cause-and-effect sentences that show how the problem is solved.

Problem: _____

_____

Solution: _____

_____

_____

_____

_____

In part **B,** you have written an outline for a story. On a separate sheet, write the story. Include dialogue and details to bring your story to life.

Many stories contain a problem and a chain of causes and effects that lead to a solution.

lesson 6 More ways to combine sentences

You can combine two sentences by using a comma and the words *and, or,* or *but.* These words are called **conjunctions,** and the resulting sentence is called a **compound sentence.** See how these compound sentences are formed.

Mrs. Jones turned off the TV. The children were shocked.
Mrs. Jones turned off the TV, <u>and</u> the children were shocked.

Mrs. Jones is happy. Brian Jones is unhappy.
Mrs. Jones is happy, <u>but</u> Brian Jones is unhappy.

You can watch TV this evening. You can read a book this evening.
You can watch TV this evening, <u>or</u> you can read a book.

Notice that *and* is used when the second sentence adds to the meaning of the first. *But* is used to show contrast. *Or* is used to show a choice.

A. Combine each pair of sentences below. Use the conjunctions *and, but,* or *or.*

1. Brian stares at the blank TV. Alvin plays with toys.

    _____

2. Maria Jones found a book. She could not read it.

    _____

3. The children can play alone. The children can play with friends.

    _____

4. The TV has been off for a week now. The children still miss it.

    _____

5. They still complain. Their mother doesn't mind.

    _____

Another way to combine two sentences is to use a **subordinate conjunction,** such as *when* or *because.* Look at the differences in these sentences.

Mrs. Jones turned off the TV, <u>and</u> the children were shocked.
<u>Because</u> Mrs. Jones turned off the TV, the children were shocked.
<u>When</u> Mrs. Jones turned off the TV, the children were shocked.

Subordinate conjunctions often show cause-and-effect or time relationships between the sentences being combined. Some subordinate conjunctions that show cause and effect are *because, since, if, so, although,* and *unless.* Some subordinate conjunctions that show time are *when, before, after,* and *while.*

B. Combine each pair of sentences below. Use a subordinate conjunction. Try to use a different subordinate conjunction in each sentence.

1. Catherine got the part. I wasn't tall enough.

   _____

2. I heard the director's choice. I was very upset.

   _____

3. Catherine got the part. I became her understudy.

   _____

4. We had been practicing for a month. Catherine broke her leg.

   _____

5. Catherine could not walk. I starred on opening night.

   _____

 Look back at the "Write On" exercises you've written for this unit. Have you used conjunctions and subordinate conjunctions to combine sentences? Choose one "Write On" paragraph or story. Underline any conjunctions you've used. Find places where adding conjunctions will help clarify your meaning or eliminate choppy sentences. Then rewrite your paragraph.

Use conjunctions and subordinate conjunctions to combine short sentences.

Proofreading

Using past-tense verb forms

The players <u>practice</u> every day.
Yesterday, they <u>practiced</u> for four hours.

Practiced is the **past tense** of the verb *practice*. You form the past tense of most verbs by adding *d* or *ed*. Here are some examples.

jump jump<u>ed</u>   dribble dribble<u>d</u>   guard guard<u>ed</u>

When a one-syllable verb ends in a single vowel followed by a single consonant, you double the consonant before adding *ed*. For example:

star star<u>red</u>   mob mob<u>bed</u>   clap clap<u>ped</u>

Many verbs have irregular past-tense forms. You can find them in your dictionary. Here are some examples.

Verb	Past	Verb	Past
ride	rode	go	went
strike	struck	bring	brought
read	read	write	wrote

A. On the line in each sentence that follows, write the past tense of the verb in parentheses. Use your dictionary to check on irregular forms if you have to.

1. Alicia and I (try) _____ to move the piano the other day.

2. We accidentally (break) _____ an expensive lamp.

3. Alicia (scrape) _____ the paint off the wall and (rip) _____ the carpet.

4. I (trip) _____ and (sprain) _____ my ankle.

5. The piano leg (fall) _____ through the floor.

6. The noise (bother) _____ my uncle, who was sleeping in the room below.

7. He (dream) _____ that he was on a ship.

8. He (think) _____ that an iceberg hit the ship.

9. So he (grab) _____ a pillow and (jump) _____ overboard.

10. He (awake) _____ on the floor.

Look at the underlined verbs in the following sentences.

Dad has worked for the city for twenty years.
I have sampled all thirty-two flavors of ice cream.

Notice that *has* and *have* are followed by forms of verbs that look like the past tense *(worked, sampled)*. For regular verbs, the form following *have* is the same as the past-tense form. But many irregular verbs have different forms after *have*. Here are a few. You will find others listed in your dictionary.

Verb	Past	Form After Have
come	came	come
eat	ate	eaten
go	went	gone
ring	rang	rung

B. Write in the correct form of the verb in parentheses for each sentence below. Use a dictionary if you need help.

1. Bjorn has _____ you a present. (bring)

2. Aunt May has _____ your favorite cake. (make)

3. Have you _____ it yet? (see)

4. Why haven't you _____ me about it? (tell)

5. The ball has _____ the window. (break)

6. Susie has _____ to try out for the class play. (decide)

7. What has Chita _____ under the bed? (hide)

8. Have you or your sister _____ on an airplane? (fly)

When you proofread your writing, check to see if:
• **you used correct past-tense forms**
• **you used correct verb forms after have or has**

Post-Test

1. Write the letter of each riddle next to the cause that explains it.

    a. Why was the rhino in an accident?

    _____ It ran around a lot but didn't go anywhere.

    b. Why did the astronaut land on the sun at night?

    _____ Its horn didn't work.

    c. Why was the fence like some people?

    _____ It was too hot during the day.

2. Use the word in parentheses to combine each pair of sentences.

    a. Silly Willy threw the clock out the window. He wanted to see time fly. (because)

    _____

    b. Our team's colors are black and blue. We lose every game. (since)

    _____

3. Combine each pair of sentences in two ways. First use the coordinate conjunctions *and*, *but*, or *or*. Then use a subordinate conjunction instead.

    a. Josh blew out the candles. Father cut the cake.

    _____

    _____

    b. Megan was wearing a mask and wig. Aunt Tess didn't recognize her.

    _____

    _____

4. Sometimes a cause will have several effects. Write a paragraph that tells at least three effects of one of the following causes.

    a. A small airplane has to land on a highway.
    b. A blizzard drops over three feet of snow on a neighborhood.
    c. A city loses its electricity for a day during a blackout.

unit 7

Making Your Point in Writing

Things to Remember About Making Your Point in Writing

The **purpose** of a piece of writing may be to inform, to entertain, to express feelings or opinions, or to persuade.

Writing
- Know your purpose before you begin to write.
- Keep in mind the audience for whom you are writing.

Revising
- Add or change modifiers. Be careful about their placement in your sentences.

Proofreading
Check to see that you have
- used an apostrophe to show where letters are left out in contractions such as *doesn't*
- used an apostrophe and an *s* to make a singular noun or plural noun not ending in *s* into a possessive
- used just an apostrophe to make a plural noun that ends in *s* into a possessive

lesson

1 Writing for a purpose

A. Imagine yourself marooned on a tiny desert island. The water is filled with hungry sharks. Since you happen to have a bottle and cork, a pencil, and a small slip of paper, you decide to send a message. What will you write?

1. Write your message on the lines below. There is room for only three sentences on your slip of paper.

_____

_____

_____

2. What is the purpose of your message?

_____

_____

In a way, writing is like sending a message in a bottle. Writers want someone to read what they've written, and they usually have a purpose for writing it. Four common purposes for writing are:

to inform or describe   to express feelings or opinions
to entertain   to persuade

B. These four messages were found in bottles. Read each and decide what the author's purpose was. Write the purpose on the line below each message.

1. The sky and sea must be happy to shine so brilliantly. The white sharks cut through the water like gleaming knives. Nothing is more wonderful than an island in the ocean.

   Purpose: _____

2. My island is 300 kilometers southwest of Australia. It is surrounded by great white sharks, also known as man-eaters. They are about six meters in length. They circle their prey several times before attacking.

   Purpose: _____

3. I offer $25,000 to the person who rescues me from this island. Please come and get me. I will make it worth your while.

   Purpose: _____

4. The ocean around my island is quite friendly—it waves all day. The sharks, however, are a worry. Of course, there is only one thing to do if you see a shark while you're swimming—hope that it doesn't see you. I bumped headfirst into a shark while swimming yesterday, and I was really *sharked!*

   Purpose: _____

Pretend you are marooned on a desert island. On a separate sheet, write each of the following:

1. a three-sentence note that describes the island
2. a short note that tells your feelings about the island and whether or not you wish to leave
3. a few sentences to the captain of a small boat that has stopped at the island, in which you try to persuade him to take you aboard
4. some jokes you would tell the captain to keep him in good spirits

---

Most writing has a purpose. Four common purposes are: to inform, to entertain, to express feelings or opinions, and to persuade.

2 Writing for an audience

DONT BE LEFT SPEECHLESS CALL ELLA Q. SHUN

Meet Ella the Speech Writer. Ella says that writing speeches is easy, once you know who your audience will be.

A. Ella has already written three speeches today. They are called:

> Growing Tulips in the Snow
> Batting Practice Can Pay Off
> Monsters for the Modern Age

The speeches will be given to the groups below. Write the name of the speech next to the group you think would be most interested in hearing it.

1. The Mudville Little League _____

2. The Horror Story Writers of America _____

3. The Garden Society of Antarctica _____

Sometimes Ella writes about different topics to suit different audiences. But even the same topic requires different kinds of information for different audiences.

B. Last week, Ella wrote two speeches about automobiles. The audiences were:

> The Sixth-Grade Science Club of Bayview School
> The National Historical Car Society

Read part of each speech below. Then decide which audience it is meant for. Write the name of the audience on the line after the speech.

1. The first Stanley Steamer had a trial run in Newton, Massachusetts, in 1897. It was driven by its designers, the Stanley twins.

   _____

2. The engine is the car's power plant. It produces the power that turns the wheels. Most cars have a gasoline engine.

   _____

C. Ella also wrote two speeches about football. One audience, an Argentine soccer club, knew nothing about American football. The other audience was the Association of American College Football Coaches. On the lines below, explain how these speeches might have been different. Give an example of the kind of information that might be given in each speech.

_____

_____

_____

_____

 Choose one of the topics below, or think up your own idea. Write two short speeches for two different audiences. Before you write each speech, indicate which audience it is for.

> Why I Enjoy My Hobby: to an audience of fellow hobbyists and to the Parent's Club
> What's Good and Bad in Our School: to the PTA and to an audience of foreign students

When you write, keep in mind the audience for whom you are writing.

3 Writing a letter of complaint

A **letter of complaint** is usually a business letter. Like all business letters, it should have an inside address (the receiver's address) and a colon after the greeting. Read the letter of complaint below.

Heading →

234 Straining Road
Huffman, Alabama
November 18, 19—

Inside → Mr. Muscles, Inc.
Address 250 Bulge Avenue
Strongman, Georgia

Greeting → Dear Mr. Muscles:

Body →

    On July 14 of this year, I ordered Body Building Kit #84 A from your company. The kit was advertised in the June 30 issue of Fathead Comix. The kit cost $14.95 and had a thirty-day, money-back guarantee. I waited three months for the kit. When it came, there were no weights or barbells, although the picture in the ad showed a man lifting weights. There was only a thick piece of elastic with handles. I have been pulling this elastic for thirty days, and I am still an eighty-pound weakling.

    Now I have returned the kit to your company. I want my money back immediately. I also think you should not show barbells in your ad if you are selling only elastic bands.

Closing →
Signature →

        Yours truly,

        Petey Weaker

        Petey Weaker

A. The body of a letter of complaint often has two parts. The first part explains what the problem is by giving facts. Read Petey's letter again and answer these questions.

   1. What did Petey Weaker buy? _____

2. When did he order it? _____

3. How much did he pay for it? _____

B. The second part of the body of a letter of complaint makes demands and/or gives suggestions. It tells what should be done to correct a situation. What demand does Petey Weaker make? What suggestions? Write these on the lines below.

_____

_____

C. Here is part of a letter of complaint that Peggy Weaker wrote to the local newspaper. She forgot to make any demands or give any suggestions. Add at least one demand and one suggestion that might help the situation.

Dear Editor:

    I live next to the Purity Chemical Company on Clearwater Road in Huffman. Every night a thick purple gas belches out of this company's smokestack. The gas sticks to everything. I can hardly breathe anymore! Purity also pumps a heavy green liquid into the Clearwater River. The water is now so thick that you can almost walk across it.

_____

_____

_____

_____

Think of a pollution problem in your town or neighborhood. It might be air, water, or noise pollution. On a separate sheet of paper, write a letter of complaint to your local newspaper or government. Follow the style of Petey's letter. Explain the problem and make suggestions.

A letter of complaint is a business letter. The body often contains two parts. One part explains the problem. The second part makes demands and/or suggestions to solve the problem.

Writing a review

People write **reviews** of books, movies, plays, and TV shows. Reviewers give their opinions about the works and suggest whether or not other people should read or see them. Here is part of a review of a new play.

Boris Knot's new play, *Dora's Dreams*, tells the story of Dora, a shop worker whose dreams make up several acts. In one scene, she is a princess in Egypt. In another, she is the first woman on the moon. But Dora always says and does the expected. The dialogue is dull and trite. The snores of many in the audience indicated that they were enjoying their own dreams through much of the play.

There were only two bright spots in the evening. One was the performance of Lana Lovely as Dora. She's obviously an actress to watch. In a better play, she'll really shine. The elaborate settings and costumes were also a joy. But if you're looking for new ideas or clever dialogue, don't bother seeing *Dora's Dreams*.

A. Look back at the review to answer the questions that follow.

1. What does the reviewer say the play is about?

_____

2. List two things the reviewer doesn't like about the play.

_____

_____

3. List two things the reviewer likes about the play.

_____

_____

4. Does the reviewer think other people should see the play? _____

B. Write the name of a play, movie, or TV show that you saw recently. Tell where and when you saw it.

_____

_____

C. Write a short paragraph that tells what the show or movie was about. Be sure not to give away the ending.

_____

_____

_____

_____

D. List a few things that you liked and a few things you didn't like about the show or movie.

_____

_____

_____

_____

On a separate sheet of paper, write a review of the show or movie you listed in part **B.** Include the short summary of the plot that you wrote for part **C.** You may wish to describe in more detail one scene that stands out in your mind. Then write your opinions of the show, the actors, the sets and costumes, and the dialogue. Use the ideas you listed in part **D.** End by telling whether or not you think others would enjoy the show.

A review usually includes a short summary of the work, the reviewer's opinions about it, and a suggestion as to whether other people should see or read it.

5 Making a poster

Originally a **poster** was a notice nailed onto a strong, high post. The letters in a poster had to be big so people could read them. The title had to be interesting to catch the attention of the people passing by. Most importantly, the poster had to tell *what* was happening, *where*, *when*, and sometimes *why*.

A. Look at the poster in the picture. Then write answers to the following *wh* questions.

What: _____

Where: _____

When: _____

B. On the lines below, write the title for a poster about one of the following events. Make the title as interesting as possible.

> a garage sale at your house
> a bicycle race through your town or neighborhood
> a costume party at your school

_____

_____

C. Make up answers to these *wh* questions for the title you wrote for part **B.**

What: _____

Where: _____

When: _____

D. The art and design of a poster are very important. Eye-catching, attractive art will make people notice your poster. Legible lettering will get your message across. In the space below, sketch a rough design of your poster. Show where the title and the information in part **C** will appear. Show where the artwork or photographs will be placed.

 Using the rough sketch from part **D** as a guide, make a real poster.

A poster tells <u>what</u>, <u>when</u>, <u>where</u> and sometimes <u>why</u>. Posters work better if they have catchy titles and are well designed.

Revising

Placing modifiers correctly

Modifiers are words or groups of words that give information and add details to a sentence. A modifier should be as close as possible to the word or words it describes. A modifier in the wrong place can cause confusion.

In the cartoon above, *named Sullivan* is a modifier. It tells about the man, not his eye. It is in the wrong place. This sentence is clearer:

"We're looking for a man named Sullivan who has one eye."

A. Find a misplaced modifier in each of the following sentences. Draw a line under it. Then, rewrite the sentence on the line so that it is clearer.

1. Bob received candy from his uncle made in Holland.

_____

2. The actors left before it began to rain in the yellow school bus.

_____

3. I read a book about training seals in the library.

_____

4. I traveled with a woman on the train with eight children.

_____

The -ing form of a verb is often used as a modifier, either alone or as part of a phrase. An -ing modifier should be as close as possible to the word or words it modifies in a sentence. If the word it modifies is missing, you will have to add it. Look at these misplaced and dangling modifiers and their corrections.

Misplaced Modifier: We saw nine swimming pools driving down the high-way.

Corrected Sentence: Driving down the highway, we saw nine swimming pools.

Dangling Modifier: Driving down the highway, a woodchuck scurried by.

Corrected Sentence: Driving down the highway, we saw a woodchuck scurry by.

B. Draw a line under the misplaced or dangling modifiers in the sentences below. Then rewrite each sentence so that the modifiers are correctly placed. Add words where necessary.

1. Screaming wildly, Mr. Fong listened to the baby.

_____

2. Soaring high above, the children waved at the hang glider.

_____

3. After drinking the milk, the glasses were put in the sink.

_____

4. After eating spinach, the dessert was a treat.

_____

Look over the papers you've written for this unit. Are any of your modifiers misplaced or dangling? Do you want to add any modifiers to give additional information or details? Choose one paper to rewrite. Add or change modifiers, but be careful of their placement.

Be sure that your modifiers aren't misplaced in a sentence.

Proofreading

Using apostrophes

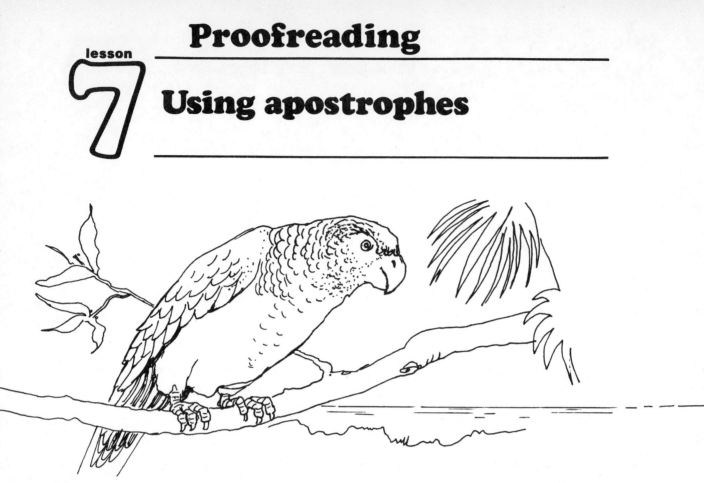

There's no sound on this island except that parrot's squawking.

Look at the **apostrophes** in the sentence above. Apostrophes are used in two ways: to form **contractions** and to form **possessives.**

   In a contraction, an apostrophe shows where a letter or letters have been left out. Look at these contractions.

there's = there is	doesn't = does not
I'll = I will	haven't = have not

Notice that in some contractions a subject and verb are combined. The first letter or letters of the verb are left out, and an apostrophe is put in their place. In other contractions, a verb is combined with *not.* In this case, the *o* of *not* is left out, forming the ending *n't.*

A. Make each pair of words below into a contraction.

1. would not _____

2. I am _____

3. do not _____

4. she is _____

5. has not _____

6. they are _____

7. are not _____

8. we will _____

Add an apostrophe and *s* to a singular noun to form a possessive:

the squawking of that parrot = that parrot's squawking
the hat Bess owns = Bess's hat

Add only an apostrophe to a plural noun that ends in *s*:

the tools of the workers = the workers' tools

But if a plural noun does not end in *s*, add an apostrophe and *s*.

the toys of the children = the children's toys

B. Rewrite each word group below to change it to a possessive phrase. Follow the examples above.

1. the trunks of the elephants = _____

2. the glasses of the teacher = _____

3. the jobs of the men = _____

4. the masks of the robbers = _____

5. the new clothes of the emperor = _____

6. the scarf Chris owns = _____

C. Rewrite the paragraph below, putting in apostrophes where they are needed.

The citizens votes arent all counted yet. Therefore the governors message wont be broadcast until later. Were wondering what hes going to say.

_____

_____

_____

When you proofread your writing, check to see that you:
- **use an apostrophe to show where letters are left out in a contraction**
- **use an apostrophe and an s to make a singular noun or plural noun not ending in s into a possessive**
- **use just an apostrophe to make a plural noun that ends in s into a possessive**

111

1. Tell whether the purpose of each sentence is to entertain, inform, give opinions, or persuade.

   a. Terriers were bred to find and scare small animals from their burrows.

   _____

   b. You couldn't buy a better pet or watchdog than a bull terrier.

   _____

   c. Our puppy is a terrier—we live in terrier of what he will chew up next.

   _____

2. Rewrite each sentence to fix the misplaced or dangling modifier.

   a. I saw a movie about sailing in that theater.

   _____

   b. Barking loudly, the children found the dog.

   _____

   c. When only three years old, my father taught me to swim.

   _____

3. In the following sentences, add apostrophes where they are needed.

   a. "I dont like Toms sherbets taste," said Sonia icily.

   b. "Its bitter and theres no sugar in it," she added sourly.

4. Write a paragraph on one of the topics listed below. The purpose of the paragraph can be to inform, entertain, express feelings or opinions, or persuade. Then write a second paragraph on the same topic. The purpose of the second paragraph should be different from the first.

   a pet   a TV show   a sport   an interesting job

unit 8

Point of View in Writing

Things to Remember About Point of View in Your Writing

A **point of view** is how someone sees or thinks about something.

Writing Tips

- Decide on your point of view before you begin writing.
- Choose the writing form that best expresses your point of view: play, poem, short story, essay, or news article.
- Use the pronouns *I*, *me*, and *my* when you write from a personal point of view.
- Use the "all-knowing" point of view when you, as narrator, take no part in the action of the story.

Revising and Proofreading Tips

Check to see that your work

- has no errors in capitalization, punctuation, modifier placement, or verb forms
- contains exact nouns, verbs, and adjectives

Writing from different perspectives

Different people view the world differently. What we see—our **perspective**—depends on who we are, where we stand, and what we look at.

A. Read the paragraphs below. Each one tells about the same event from a different perspective. On the lines after each, write one or two sentences that tell who and where each speaker is and how the speaker feels.

1. OK, Wiggles, sorry to have to do this, but Old Trout loves something wet and squirming at sunup. And I want him on my table, by hook or crook. Off you go! Now find me a big one.

   _____

   _____

   _____

2. Aaaaoouch! That's my skin, buster! Glub . . . glub . . . glub. . . . Just my luck to get caught in the middle of their game. One pokes holes in me and tries to drown me, and then the other bites my head off.

   _____

   _____

   _____

3. Hmmmmmmmmmm. That looks like the shadow of Fred Kowalski's boat up there on the surface. He's up early—up to no good, that is. And what's an earthworm doing in my lake anyway? Something's fishy here.

   _____

B. What ball game do you most enjoy playing or watching—baseball, basketball, tennis, or something else? Write a few sentences about a ball game from the point of view of a player or a viewer.

_____

_____

_____

_____

C. Now write about the same game from the point of view of the ball.

_____

_____

_____

_____

Choose one of the situations below. On another sheet of paper, write one paragraph from each perspective mentioned in the situation.
1. a family making a long drive to the mountains for a vacation, from the perspective of a child eager to arrive, and from the perspective of the car making the trip
2. a game-winning home run, from the perspective of the happy batter who hit the ball, and from that of the sad pitcher who threw it
3. a mouse hunt, from the perspective of a cat trying to catch the mouse, and from that of the mouse trying to avoid being caught

A perspective depends on one's point of view. You can write about the same situation from different perspectives.

2 Writing in different forms

There are different forms of written composition. Some common forms are **plays, poems, short stories, essays,** and **newspaper articles.** A writer chooses the form that is best suited for expressing his or her point of view.

A **play** is usually written to be performed on a stage. A play includes characters and a setting. The special form of a play contains directions to the actors as well as the lines they speak. Read this portion of a play.

SCENE: *A farm. A large barn stands in the center of the stage. A boy and girl are painting the barn, but only a small section is done. They look discouraged.*

KEN *(painting):* We'll never finish this barn before sundown.

HELGA *(wiping brow and looking over barn):* I know. We promised Dad we'd finish before school starts again, and that's tomorrow.

KEN: With just the two of us, it's an impossible task.

HELGA: Wait a minute! *(She puts down her brush and claps her hands.)* I have a great idea!

A. Write an additional line of dialogue for each character. Include directions for the actors. Follow the sample above.

KEN: _____

_____

HELGA: _____

_____

Poetry is imaginative writing that expresses experience through the meaning, sound, and/or rhythm of words. Poems are written in many different forms. One form is the **cinquain.** It is a five-line poem in which each line has a specific number of syllables. Look at this example.

In fall	(2 syllables)
The days get short.	(4 syllables)
Big orange pumpkins come	(6 syllables)
Tree leaves turn yellow-brown, and fall	(8 syllables)
In fall.	(2 syllables)

B. Write a cinquain about something you have seen lately. It could be about something in nature or something manufactured.

_____

_____

_____

_____

_____

Write about the scene above. Write a poem, a play, a short story, or some other form of composition. Choose the form that will best express your point of view.

Some common writing forms are plays, poems, short stories, essays, and newspaper articles. You can choose the form which best expresses your point of view.

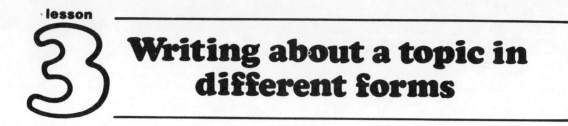

3 Writing about a topic in different forms

Similar ideas can be expressed in different forms. Read this **limerick**.

> There was an old man with a beard,
> Who said, "It is just as I feared!
> Two owls and a hen
> Four larks and a wren
> Have all built their nests in my beard."

> —*Edward Lear*

A. Pretend you are a reporter for a local newspaper. Write a news story about the man in the poem. Be sure to make up answers to the *wh* questions.

_____

_____

_____

_____

_____

Read the following passage from a play.

SETTING: *The Starship Nexus in flight to Galaxy 11.*

FIRST ASSISTANT *(staring through stellascope):* Captain! A meteor shower! We'll be killed!

CAPTAIN PORTUS *(sternly):* Raise the deflectors! Dr. Desidero, what are our coordinates?

DOCTOR DESIDERO: You must turn this ship around, or it will be too late.

CAPTAIN PORTUS *(angrily):* I asked for the coordinates, Dr. Desidero. *(The star ship rocks violently; Captain Portus is thrown to the ground.)*

FIRST ASSISTANT: Captain!

DR. DESIDERO: Leave him alone. I am in charge now.

B. How would you give this same information in the form of a short story? Write a paragraph from your story. Try not to leave out any information that is in the play.

_____

_____

_____

_____

_____

_____

_____

 An essay is a composition that deals with a topic from a personal point of view. Read this section of an essay. Can you express the same feelings in the form of a short poem? Write your poem on another sheet of paper.

My wise mother turned me loose in the country and let me run wild, learning from nature what no books can teach. I remember running over the hills just at dawn one summer morning. Pausing to rest, I saw the sun rise over river, hill, and wide green meadows as I had never seen it before. Those days were the happiest of my life.

—_Louisa May Alcott_

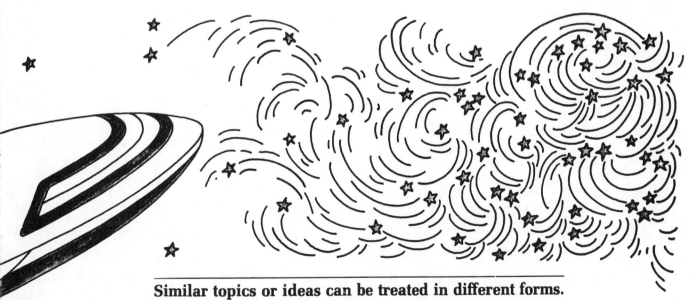

Similar topics or ideas can be treated in different forms.

Narrating a story

Every story has an author. The author decides from whose point of view the story will be told, or **narrated.** Sometimes an author uses a character in the story as the narrator. We say this type of story is told from a **personal point of view.** You can recognize the personal point of view by the use of the pronouns *I, me,* and *my.*

Read this portion of a story. It is told from a personal point of view.

> At eleven one night I was riding home along the old railroad-yard road near Waterton. My motorcycle sputtered and died. I was out of gas—in the middle of nowhere. I was telling myself how stupid I was when I heard the wolf howl.

A. Pretend you are narrating this story. Write several sentences from a personal point of view to continue the story.

_____

_____

_____

_____

_____

Often, the writer serves as the narrator, taking no part in the action of the story. In this case, the narrator seems to know everything about the characters, the setting, and the plot. This type of narrator tells the story from an **"all-knowing" point of view.**

Read this portion of a story. Think about who is telling the story.

The old woman stared carefully at the sign: Police Headquarters. Then she strode into the reception room. In her right hand she clutched a yellow parking ticket.

The sergeant sat behind a high green desk. He frowned when he saw her. He had not had a very good day so far.

"Yes?" he asked, looking up from his blotter.

"Excuse me," the woman began. . . .

"What is it?" the sergeant snapped.

"Did one of your officers lose this?" she said, holding up the ticket. "I just found it lying on the windshield of my car."

B. Write a few more lines to this story. Your lines should continue telling the story from an "all-knowing" point of view.

_____

_____

_____

_____

_____

_____

 Write about a dream you have had. Tell about it from a personal point of view. After you have written down the dream, think about how you could change it into a story. Write a story based on the dream. Make whatever changes you wish. Tell the story from an "all-knowing" point of view.

Stories can be told from a personal point of view or an "all-knowing" point of view.

Revising and Proofreading

Polishing your writing

When you have finished writing, you should **proofread** your work to correct any errors in capitalization, commas, end punctuation, apostrophes, modifier placement, verb forms, and so on. You may also revise your work. To **revise** means to rewrite with improvements. When you revise, you may choose more exact nouns, verbs, or adjectives. You may add adverbial phrases. You may combine sentences to improve paragraph rhythm or to clarify your meaning.

A. Follow the directions listed below this paragraph in order to revise it. Write your new paragraph on the blank lines.

    The streets were crowded. They were narrow. Filling the air, we heard music, sounds of laughter, and cheerful greetings. Shoppers went from store to store. Someone dropped a lot of gaily wrapped packages. Many people rushed over to help. We all felt the joyful holiday spirit.

1. Combine the first two sentences.
2. Change the misplaced modifier in sentence 3.
3. Use a more interesting verb in sentence 4.
4. Make the subject of sentence 5 more exact.
5. Combine sentences 5 and 6.

_____

_____

_____

_____

_____

_____

_____

_____

B. Revise the next paragraph yourself. Try to make each subject and verb exact. Combine some sentences, and watch for dangling or misplaced modifiers.

The car came down the street. It stopped. The man asked for directions leaning out of the car. A woman was on the sidewalk. On a leash she had a dog. She told him something. He drove away.

_____

_____

_____

_____

_____

_____

Find one "Write On" paragraph you wrote in this unit that could use revising. On another sheet of paper, rewrite the paragraph. Think about sentence length, exact words, position of modifiers, and so on. Ask yourself if your paragraph says exactly what you want it to say.

Revise your writing until it says exactly what you want it to say.

Post-Test

1. The following points of view were expressed in a busy store. Write the letter of each point of view next to the person who would hold it.

   a. I love crowds like this! I make so much money.

   _____ a shopper

   b. Look at these crowds! I won't get a minute to relax.

   _____ the store owner

   c. Look at these crowds! I think I'll come back some other time.

   _____ a clerk in the store

2. Rewrite this story paragraph in play form.

   The director angrily asked the actor if he had acting experience. The actor nodded confidently and said his leg had been in a cast.

   _____

   _____

3. Revise this paragraph. Use the rules you've learned.

   A truck full of pigs was speeding down a road. It skid on some ice. It turned over. Squealing on the road, we saw dozens of pigs running away. Someone came to help.

   _____

   _____

   _____

4. On a separate piece of paper, rewrite the paragraph above from the truck driver's point of view. Then rewrite it again from one of the pig's point of view. Add an ending to the story in each paragraph.

Unit 1

Lesson 1 (pages 2–3)

A. 🔲 Whenever you see this symbol, check with your teacher.

B. You should have underlined the first sentence.

C. Your answer should be similar to this: *A creature like Big Foot seems to be living in this area.*

Lesson 2 (pages 4–5)

A. 🔲

B. For the first paragraph, you should have underlined the first sentence. You should have crossed out: *Everyone played softball, and there were pony rides for the kids. I once got sick from eating egg salad.*
For the second paragraph, you should have underlined the first sentence. You should have crossed out: *She has nice dark hair that she wears long. I like my hair short.*

Lesson 3 (pages 6–7)

A. 🔲 **B.** 🔲 **C.** 🔲

Lesson 4 (pages 8–9)

A. Did you include the tracks of people, sleds, dogs, a horse, and someone on crutches?

B. 🔲 Were you able to guess what these objects really are? Here are the real answers. The first object, a pannier, is a frame worn under a woman's dress to enlarge the dress around the hips. The second object, a candle mold, was used to make candles. The wick was threaded through the mold. Then hot wax was poured into the mold and allowed to cool. The third object, a bed warmer, was used to warm up the bed on a chilly night. Hot coals were placed in the pan to give off heat.

Lesson 5 (pages 10–11)

A. 1. Who: George McJunkin
    When: 1925
    Where: Folsom, New Mexico
    What: found unusual bones and a stone spearhead
  2. Who: scientists at a nearby university
    What: were very surprised at the discovery
    Why: They realized that people had lived in America 8,000 years ago.

B. 🔲

Lesson 6 (pages 12–13)

A. You might have used these exact nouns:
  1. Saint Bernard   3. fruit salad
  2. daisies   4. shriek   5. sports car

B. 🔲 **C.** 🔲

Lesson 7 (pages 14–15)

A. 1. 1 and 2   3. Kristie, Robin   5. no
  2. 3 and 4   4. walked, ran   6. no

B. a subject and a verb

C. 1. S   5. N   8. S
  2. N   6. S   9. N
  3. N   7. N   10. N
  4. S

D. The cook stirred the mixture ᵀ then he poured it into a baking dish. He ᵖᵘᵗ it into the oven. When do ʸᵒᵘ think it will be ready?

Unit 2

Lesson 1 (pages 18–19)

A. First: Mix two parts water with one part flour.
  Next: Stir until the mixture is smooth, sticky, and wet.
  Third: Dip the strips of newspaper into the mixture.
  Finally: Apply the strips to the form.

B. 🔲

C. You might have written:
First move all the furniture out of the room. Next sweep and wash the entire floor. Then begin painting from one corner of the room, working your way towards the door. Finally step outside the doorway and paint the remaining section near the door.

Lesson 2 (pages 20–21)

A. Go north on Route 27. Take Bike Trail on right to Woodland Road. Go east on Woodland, past Glen Court, to Spruce Street. Turn right on Spruce to Foot Path on left. Take Foot Path to Campsite.

B. Holly went past Shifting Sands and kept to the right. She passed the Lake of Howling Trees. At the fork, she went left and passed Deep Holes. She took the left fork again, passed the Volcano and Wall of Vengeance to the Shuttle.

Lesson 3 (pages 22–23)

A. 5, 1, 2, 6, 3, 4, 7   **B.** 🔲   **C.** 🔲

Lesson 4 (pages 24–25)

A. A man in the desert calls for water. A trader passes, trying to sell him a tie. The man cries, "Water . . . water," and crawls on. The trader comes back and offers him a tie, saying, "At half price, it's a steal." But the man goes on until he sees a hotel. As he crawls up to the door, the doorman says, "I'm sorry, Sir. No one's allowed in without a tie."

B. 3, 2, 4, 1
Hey, did you ever hear this one? A woman goes into a diner and orders a cup of coffee. She takes a sip and screams, "This coffee tastes like mud." The waiter says, "Well, it was ground this morning."

Lesson 5 (pages 26–27)

A. I. What is it?
    A. Appearance

125

1. Hairy body and face like person
2. Walks erect on thick legs
   B. Where it is found
      1. Lives in Mount Everest and other Himalaya mountains
      2. Sometimes seen near villages
   II. Does it really exist?
      A. Expeditions
         1. Several expeditions have searched for the beast.
         2. In 1951, a British explorer took pictures of "snowman" tracks.
      B. Explanations
         1. The beast may simply be a large bear.
         2. When bear tracks in snow melt, they may look like huge footprints.

B. ⇨

Lesson 6 (pages 28–29)

A. ⇨   **B.** ⇨   **C.** ⇨

Lesson 7 (pages 30–31)

A. ⇨
B. Did you put in these capital letters?
1. Kermit, Quake Lake
2. Miyamoto, Saturn, Thursday
3. Julia Chicken, Tuesday
4. Black, Painted Desert
5. Detroit, Friday, December
6. Northfield School, Columbus Day
7. Tower of Pizza, Poplar Street, Newburgh
8. Jason's Mart, Election Day
C. ⇨

Unit **3**

Lesson 1 (pages 34–35)

A. bigger   greener
more colorful   more delicious
B. ⇨   **C.** ⇨

Lesson 2 (pages 36–37)

A. ⇨
B. You might have said:

1776	1976
sailing ship	tugboat
a few small buildings	many skyscrapers
trees	no trees
open spaces	no open space

Lesson 3 (pages 38–39)

A. You might have said:
1. They both contain words. Both are made of paper.
2. They both have a sharp point. Both are long and thin.
3. They are both round. Both break easily.
4. They both have a beginning and an end. Both contain a series of events.
B. Both fly. Both have a similar shape. Both have wide wings that move them through the air.

Lesson 4 (pages 40–41)

A. 1. cheeks, roses   2. nose, cherry

126

3. beard, snow   5. belly, jelly
4. smoke, wreath

B. ⇨   **C.** ⇨

Lesson 5 (pages 42–43)

A. 1. classroom—zoo   2. ghost—moon
B. ⇨   **C.** ⇨

Lesson 6 (pages 44–45)

A. You might have listed *unsmiling, hooked nose, long chin, receding hair, big ears, wrinkled clothes.*
B. You should have underlined:
   1. rasping   3. crumpled   5. choppy,
   2. dangerous   4. jerky   nervous
C. ⇨

Lesson 7 (pages 46–47)

A. 1. old, rickety
2. knocked, banged, and pushed
3. high, squeaky
4. a table, a chair, and a saucer of milk
5. small, skinny
B. 1. No, Oakland, California
2. Kim, 95 Birch Lane, Oakdale, Pennsylvania
3. April 14, 1979
4. October 9, 1976
5. Yes, Bert, Mexico City, Mexico
C. Your corrected paragraph should look like this:
   Yes, Jack, I lost my wallet, my money, and my keys. I can't get into my house at 37 Lombard Street, Columbus, Ohio. Can you help me?

Unit **4**

Lesson 1 (pages 50–51)

A. chimera, manticore, leucocrotta
B. The chimera has the head of a lion, the shaggy body and hoofs of a goat, and the tail of a dragon.
C. ⇨

Lesson 2 (pages 52–53)

A. You might have listed:
flat roof   overgrown lawn
one chimney   house next door
small porch
B. ⇨

Lesson 3 (pages 54–55)

A. ⇨   **B.** ⇨   **C.** ⇨   **D.** ⇨

Lesson 4 (pages 56–57)

A. Did you check the picture on the right?
B. ⇨
C. handsome and clever, has had an easy life
D. ⇨

Lesson 5 (pages 58–59)

A. ⇨   **B.** ⇨

Lesson 6 (pages 60–61)

A. ⇨   **B.** ⇨
C. You might have written:

1. shouted shrilly
2. stammered bewilderedly

Lesson 7 (pages 62–63)

A. 1. "Where were you at 12:30 on the morning of the twenty-third?" asked the lawyer.
2. "I was in the kitchen," said the witness.
3. "And what were you doing there?" he cried.
4. "I was making a . . . a . . . chicken sandwich," she stammered.
5. "Exactly what did you put in your chicken sandwich, Mrs. Kelp?" asked the lawyer, with a triumphant gleam in his eye.
6. The witness licked her lips nervously and whispered, "Watercress, salt, and butter."

B. ▷▱

Unit 5

Lesson 1 (pages 66–67)

A. 1. Shana   2. Jane
3. You should have underlined: *horrible, awful, hate, unpleasant, bad, terrible*

B. You should have used three of the facts and opinions that follow.
1. The Ritz is located at 52 Bogview Road. It has a new show every week. Tonight *Under the Weather* is playing. The showings are at 8:00 and 10:00 P.M.
2. The Ritz is Bogville's finest movie theater. *Under the Weather* is an exciting new hit. You will relax in our delightfully air-cooled theater. Sink into our comfortable seats.

C. You might have said:
The food at Bogview School is not nourishing or well-prepared. The students don't like the food at Bogview School.

Lesson 2 (pages 68–69)

A. Who: Thaddeus Koslowitz
What: reported seeing an unidentified flying object
When: at midnight on October 8
Where: in the north field of Meadow Farm

B. You should have underlined these opinion words: *strange, scared, surprised.*

C. Why: The UFO was a blimp on which a disc jockey was playing music.

D. ▷▱

Lesson 3 (pages 70–71)

A. ▷▱   **B.** ▷▱

Lesson 4 (pages 72–73)

A. ▷▱   **B.** ▷▱

Lesson 5 (pages 74–75)

A. 1. B
2. You could have listed any sentence from B.
3. A
4. The myth tells a story to explain how a rainbow was created. The reasons given in the myth are not based on scientific fact.

B. ▷▱

Lesson 6 (pages 76–77)

A. 1. The bus was crowded and dirty.
2. The mountains and the sky were blue.
3. The river flows restlessly and rapidly.
4. Mirra opened one eye and yawned.
5. Leslie ran to the door and opened it.

B. 1. That pink dress is attractive.
2. That tall boy plays basketball.
3. My brand-new sweater is already dirty.

C. You might have written:
The woman sighed and shuffled her feet. She looked at the huge clock on the wall. The woman was impatient and nervous. Suddenly she heard a soft noise behind her. She jumped up and ran to the door.

Lesson 7 (pages 78–79)

A. 1. s   2. plain
B. You should have underlined
1. jog   3. goes   5. take   7. smile, wave
2. runs   4. scurry   6. pass

C. 1. am   3. are   5. are
2. is   4. are

D. ▷▱

Unit 6

Lesson 1 (pages 82–83)

A. a. 2   b. 4   c. 1   d. 3
B. You might have written:
1. Two groups of children are playing tug of war by a mud puddle. One group lands in the mud puddle.
2. Three children are high on a seasaw. When the dog sits on that side too, it goes down.

C. ▷▱

Lesson 2 (pages 84–85)

A. 1. Did you underline *therefore?* Did you circle *I know you really want to be a truckdriver?*
2. Did you underline *since?* Did you circle *it hasn't been made up yet?*
3. Did you underline *because?* Did you circle *there is a mile between its first and last letter?*
4. Did you underline *consequently?* Did you circle *Every player insists on raising a racket?*
5. Did you underline *due to?* Did you circle *the very cold temperature of the lake water?*

B. 1. Since the restaurant was on the moon, it had very little atmosphere.
2. Johnny told his mother he didn't want to write clearly because then the teacher would know he couldn't spell.
3. The rooster couldn't figure out where the sun went at night. Therefore, he stayed up until it finally dawned on him.

C. ▷▱

Lesson 3 (pages 86–87)

A. 1. Water vapor in the air freezes and forms crystals.
2. An explosive noise is caused by the sudden expansion of air heated by lightning.

127

B. 1. move the front wheel to face in a different direction
   2. turn the wheels
   3. the bike will stop
C. 1. change to snow or sleet
   2. change color or fall off the trees
   3. burn
   4. sink to the bottom

Lesson 4 (pages 88–89)

A.
B. You might have written:
   1. forced smile, looking over his shoulder nervously, package stuffed inside his jacket, big black car with out-of-state plates
   2.

Lesson 5 (pages 90–91)

A. 1. The ox began to drink the water.
   2. The water began to quench the fire.
   3. The fire began to burn the stick.
   4. The stick began to beat the dog.
   5. The dog began to bite the pig.
   6. The pig climbed over the fence.
   7. They both went home.
B.

Lesson 6 (pages 92–93)

A. You might have written:
   1. Brian stares at the blank TV, and Alvin plays with toys.
   2. Maria Jones found a book, but she could not read it.
   3. The children can play alone, or the children can play with friends.
   4. The TV has been off for a week now, and the children still miss it.
   5. They still complain, but their mother doesn't mind.
B. You might have said:
   1. Catherine got the part because I wasn't tall enough.
   2. When I heard the director's choice, I was very upset.
   3. After Catherine got the part, I became her understudy.
   4. When we had been practicing for a month, Catherine broke her leg.
   5. Because Catherine could not walk, I starred on opening night.

Lesson 7 (pages 94–95)

A. 1. tried   6. bothered
   2. broke   7. dreamed
   3. scraped, ripped 8. thought
   4. tripped, sprained 9. grabbed, jumped
   5. fell   10. awoke
B. 1. brought   5. broken
   2. made   6. decided
   3. seen   7. hidden
   4. told   8. flown

128

Unit 7

Lesson 1 (pages 98–99)

A. 1.   2. to get help
B. 1. to express feelings or opinions
   2. to inform or describe
   3. to persuade
   4. to entertain

Lesson 2 (pages 100–101)

A. 1. Batting Practice Can Pay Off
   2. Monsters for the Modern Age
   3. Growing Tulips in the Snow
B. 1. The National Historical Car Society
   2. The Sixth-Grade Science Club of Bayview School
C.

Lesson 3 (pages 102–103)

A. 1. Petey bought Body Building Kit #84A.
   2. He ordered it on July 14.
   3. He paid $14.95 for the kit.
B. Petey demanded his money back. He suggested not showing the barbells in the ad.
C.

Lesson 4 (pages 104–105)

A. 1. The play is about the dreams of Dora, a shop girl.
   2. The reviewer feels that Dora always says and does the expected. The reviewer doesn't like the dialogue.
   3. The reviewer likes the performance of Lana Lovely. The reviewer likes the elaborate settings and costumes.
   4. No.
B.   C.   D.

Lesson 5 (pages 106–107)

A. What: A horse sale
   Where: B Bar B Ranch
   When: Saturday, May 5, at noon
B.   C.   D.

Lesson 6 (pages 108–109)

A. 1. You should have underlined: *made in Holland.*
   Bob received candy made in Holland from his uncle.
   2. Underline: *in the yellow schoolbus.*
   The actors left in the yellow schoolbus before it began to rain.
   3. Underline: *in the library.*
   I read a book in the library about training seals.
   4. Underline: *with eight children.*
   On the train, I traveled with a woman with eight children.
B. 1. You should have underlined: *Screaming wildly.*
   Mr. Fong listened to the baby screaming wildly.

Lesson 7 (pages 110-111)

A.
1. wouldn't
2. I'm
3. don't
4. she's
5. hasn't
6. they're
7. aren't
8. we'll

B.
1. the elephant's trunks
2. the teacher's glasses
3. the men's jobs
4. the robbers' masks
5. the emperor's new clothes
6. Chris's scarf

C. The citizens' votes aren't all counted yet. Therefore the governor's message won't be broadcast until later. We're wondering what he's going to say.

UNIT 8

Lesson 1 (pages 114-115)

A. You should have written:
1. fisherman
2. worm
3. fish

B.   **C.**

Lesson 2 (pages 116-117)

A.   **B.**

Lesson 3 (pages 118-119)

A.   **B.**

Lesson 4 (pages 120-121)

A.   **B.**

Lesson 5 (pages 122-123)

A. You might have written:

The narrow streets were crowded. We heard music, sounds of laughter, and cheerful greetings filling the air. Shoppers bustled from store to store. A well-dressed young woman dropped a lot of gaily wrapped packages. Many people rushed over to help, because we all felt the joyful holiday spirit.

Post-Test Answers; pg 16

1. a. catcher   e. schooner
   b. apricot   f. collie
   c. grandson   g. eggplant
   d. leopard   h. pliers
2. *Topic sentence:* There are several stories about how May was named.
   Sentence that doesn't fit: Diana is the Roman goddess of hunting.
3. The hum of a mosquito is the sound of its wings beating. <u>A</u> mosquito's wings move about a thousand times a second. A female's wings <u>have</u> a higher tone than a male's wings. Why is that? <u>It</u> helps males find mates.
4. Be sure that students have chosen one of the given sentences, replacing *person, thing,* or *place* with a specific noun or even a proper noun. They may reword the idea when they write their topic sentences, but the substance should remain the same. The topic sentence should appear somewhere in the paragraph, and the other sentences should all develop the topic.

Post-Test Answers; pg 32

1. a. 3 b. 2 c. 1 d. 4
2. a. 3 b. 1 c. 5 d. 2 e. 4
3. a. stroll   d. chatter
   b. broil   e. dart
   c. gulp   f. giggle
4. a. Monday, May, Richard Powers, Chicago, Illinois
   b. Sheraton Hotel, Sears Tower
5. The students' outlines need only contain the Roman numeral and capital letter heads. If students have used numerals, check to see that they have followed standard outline form. Make sure the students' paragraphs follow the outlines they have written. The events described in the paragraphs should follow in a logical order. Check that each paragraph has a topic sentence and sentences that give details.

Post-Test Answers; pg 48

1. a. heartier, heartiest
   b. more intelligent, most intelligent
   c. smoother, smoothest
2. Answers will vary. Possible answers include:
   Similar: both have tires; both used for transportation; both must be steered; both travel on roads; both made of steel.
   Different: A car is much faster than a bicycle. A car has four wheels and a bicycle has only two. Cars are more expensive than bicycles and much larger. Accept all legitimate similarities and differences.
3. a. M
   b. S
   c. S
4. a. uninteresting
   b. colorful
   c. experienced
5. Check to see that the student has written two paragraphs, the first listing how the objects are similar and the second listing their differences. Each paragraph should have a topic sentence. The obvious similarities and differences for each pair are listed below. Students' answers will vary, however, so accept all legitimate responses.
   a horse and a camel
   Similar: Both are four-legged animals. People use both for transportation and for carrying things. Both animals can run fast and are strong. The diet of both animals is made up largely of grains and grasses.
   Different: Camels live primarily in desert areas, while horses are found almost everywhere. Camels can cover great distances without water because of their humps. Horses must drink more frequently. Horses are faster than camels and are easily trained to pull wagons and equipment.
   a radio and a TV
   Similar: Both are important forms of communication. They provide entertainment and information. Both are electronic devices. Both are receivers of signals broadcast over the air. Both have various channels.
   Different: Radios are more common because they are cheaper. Radios are usually more portable, too. Radio is an older medium than television.
   a school and a house
   Similar: Both are buildings that have walls, doors, windows, a roof, etc. People spend their time in both buildings. Both buildings are divided into rooms that have different purposes. Both are usually surrounded by a yard.
   Different: Schools are for learning, while houses are for living. Schools are usually occupied only during the day. Schools are larger than houses. Schools employ many people while houses do not. People who are related live in houses, while schools accept everyone from the community.

Post-Test Answers; pg 64

1. a
2. a. touch   b. taste
3. Any adverb or adverbial phrase is correct as long as it correctly answers the question in parentheses.
4. A man took a sip of coffee. "Yucch!" he said. "This coffee tastes like mud."
   "It should," said the waitress. "It was ground this morning."
5. You might want to bring these objects into class and display them as the students write. If you wish, permit students to write about other items that strike their fancy. Check to make sure each paragraph has a topic sentence and an adequate number of details.

Post-Test Answers; pg 80

1. a. F   c. F
   b. O   d. O
2. Students may say that Robert Jones is a good, successful, or popular author.
3. a. One cup and two plates were broken.
   b. The rains poured down and washed away our tent.
   c. The hungry alligator is next to your legs.
4. a. plays   c. like
   b. hurry   d. hears
5. You might want to have the students identify the opinion and facts in their paragraphs, perhaps by underlining or by making notations in the margin. Check to make sure the students' facts are indeed facts and that they support the stated opinion.

Post-Test Answers; pg 96

1. c
   a
   b
2. a. Silly Willy threw the clock out the window because he wanted to see time fly.
   b. Since we lose every game, our team's colors are black and blue.
3. a. Josh blew out the candles, and (but) Father cut the cake.
   After Josh blew out the candles, Father cut the cake.
   b. Megan was wearing a mask and wig, and Aunt Tess didn't recognize her. Since Megan was wearing a mask and wig, Aunt Tess didn't recognize her.
4. Make sure that the effects the students have included in their paragraphs are logical and likely effects of the cause they have chosen. Also check that the students have written topic sentences in the paragraphs.

Post-Test Answers; pg 112

1. a. inform
   b. persuade
   c. entertain
2. a. I saw a movie in that theater about sailing.
   b. The children found the dog that was barking loudly.
   c. When I was only three years old, my father taught me to swim.
3. a. "I don't like Tom's sherbet's taste," said Sonia icily.
   b. "It's bitter and there's no sugar in it," she added sourly.
4. Have the students identify the purpose of each of their paragraphs. Make sure that the sentences in each paragraph help fulfill the paragraph's purpose.

Post-Test Answers; pg 124

1. c
   a
   b
2. DIRECTOR (angrily): Have you ever had any acting experience?
   ACTOR (nodding confidently): Yes! My leg was once in a cast.
3. Revisions may vary somewhat from this: A stock truck full of pigs was speeding down Route 78, when it skidded on some ice and turned over. Dozens of pigs were running and squealing on the road. Then a nearby farmer came over to help catch the pigs.
4. Make sure the students have rewritten the paragraphs from the two different points of view. Check that the students have added endings, too. You might want to return the papers to the students for further revisions.

SPECTRUM

All our workbooks meet school curriculum guidelines and correspond to
The McGraw-Hill Companies classroom textbooks.

DOLCH Sight Word Activities

The DOLCH Sight Word Activities workbooks use the classic Dolch list of 220 basic vocabulary words that make up from 50% to 75% of all reading matter that children ordinarily encounter. Since these words are ordinarily recognized on sight, they are called *sight words*. Volume 1 includes 110 sight words. Volume 2 covers the remainder of the list. 160 pages. Answer key included.

TITLE	ISBN	PRICE
Grades K-1 Vol. 1	1-56189-917-8	$9.95
Grades K-1 Vol. 2	1-56189-918-6	$9.95

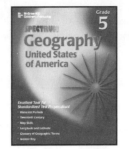

GEOGRAPHY

Full-color, three-part lessons strengthen geography knowledge and map reading skills. Focusing on five geographic themes including location, place, human/environmental interaction, movement, and regions. Over 150 pages. Glossary of geographical terms and answer key included.

TITLE	ISBN	PRICE
Grade 3, Communities	1-56189-963-1	$8.95
Grade 4, Regions	1-56189-964-X	$8.95
Grade 5, USA	1-56189-965-8	$8.95
Grade 6, World	1-56189-966-6	$8.95

MATH

Features easy-to-follow instructions that give students a clear path to success. This series has comprehensive coverage of the basic skills, helping children to master math fundamentals. Over 150 pages. Answer key included.

TITLE	ISBN	PRICE
Grade K	1-56189-900-3	$8.95
Grade 1	1-56189-901-1	$8.95
Grade 2	1-56189-902-X	$8.95
Grade 3	1-56189-903-8	$8.95
Grade 4	1-56189-904-6	$8.95
Grade 5	1-56189-905-4	$8.95
Grade 6	1-56189-906-2	$8.95
Grade 7	1-56189-907-0	$8.95
Grade 8	1-56189-908-9	$8.95

PHONICS/WORD STUDY

Provides everything children need to build multiple skills in language. Focusing on phonics, structural analysis, and dictionary skills, this series also offers creative ideas for using phonics and word study skills in other language areas. Over 200 pages. Answer key included.

TITLE	ISBN	PRICE
Grade K	1-56189-940-2	$8.95
Grade 1	1-56189-941-0	$8.95
Grade 2	1-56189-942-9	$8.95
Grade 3	1-56189-943-7	$8.95
Grade 4	1-56189-944-5	$8.95
Grade 5	1-56189-945-3	$8.95
Grade 6	1-56189-946-1	$8.95

ENRICHMENT MATH AND READING

Books in this series offer advanced math and reading for students excelling in grades 3–6. Lessons follow the same curriculum children are being taught in school while presenting the material in a way that children feel challenged. 160 pages. Answer key included.

TITLE	ISBN	PRICE
Grade 3	1-57768-503-2	$8.95
Grade 4	1-57768-504-0	$8.95
Grade 5	1-57768-505-9	$8.95
Grade 6	1-57768-506-7	$8.95

Prices subject to change without notice.

READING

This full-color series creates an enjoyable reading environment, even for below-average readers. Each book contains captivating content, colorful characters, and compelling illustrations, so children are eager to find out what happens next. Over 150 pages. Answer key included.

TITLE	ISBN	PRICE
Grade K	1-56189-910-0	$8.95
Grade 1	1-56189-911-9	$8.95
Grade 2	1-56189-912-7	$8.95
Grade 3	1-56189-913-5	$8.95
Grade 4	1-56189-914-3	$8.95
Grade 5	1-56189-915-1	$8.95
Grade 6	1-56189-916-X	$8.95

SPELLING

This full-color series links spelling to reading and writing, and increases skills in words and meanings, consonant and vowel spellings, and proofreading practice. Over 200 pages. Speller dictionary and answer key included.

TITLE	ISBN	PRICE
Grade 1	1-56189-921-6	$8.95
Grade 2	1-56189-922-4	$8.95
Grade 3	1-56189-923-2	$8.95
Grade 4	1-56189-924-0	$8.95
Grade 5	1-56189-925-9	$8.95
Grade 6	1-56189-926-7	$8.95

WRITING

Lessons focus on creative and expository writing using clearly stated objectives and pre-writing exercises. Eight essential reading skills are applied. Activities include main idea, sequence, comparison, detail, fact and opinion, cause and effect, making a point, and point of view. Over 130 pages. Answer key included.

TITLE	ISBN	PRICE
Grade 1	1-56189-931-3	$8.95
Grade 2	1-56189-932-1	$8.95
Grade 3	1-56189-933-X	$8.95
Grade 4	1-56189-934-8	$8.95
Grade 5	1-56189-935-6	$8.95
Grade 6	1-56189-936-4	$8.95
Grade 7	1-56189-937-2	$8.95
Grade 8	1-56189-938-0	$8.95

TEST PREP

Prepares children to do their best on current editions of the five major standardized tests. Activities reinforce test-taking skills through examples, tips, practice, and timed exercises. Subjects include reading, math, language arts, writing, social studies, and science. Over 150 pages. Answer key included.

TITLE	ISBN	PRICE
Grades 1-2	1-57768-672-1	$9.95
Grade 3	1-57768-673-X	$9.95
Grade 4	1-57768-674-8	$9.95
Grade 5	1-57768-675-6	$9.95
Grade 6	1-57768-676-4	$9.95
Grade 7	1-57768-677-2	$9.95
Grade 8	1-57768-678-0	$9.95

LANGUAGE ARTS

Encourages creativity and builds confidence by making writing fun! Seventy-two four-part lessons strengthen writing skills by focusing on parts of speech, word usage, sentence structure, punctuation, and proofreading. Each level includes a Writer's Handbook at the end of the book that offers writing tips. This series is based on the highly respected SRA/McGraw-Hill language arts series. More than 180 full-color pages. Answer key included.

TITLE	ISBN	PRICE
Grade 2	1-56189-952-6	$8.95
Grade 3	1-56189-953-4	$8.95
Grade 4	1-56189-954-2	$8.95
Grade 5	1-56189-955-0	$8.95
Grade 6	1-56189-956-9	$8.95

Prices subject to change without notice.

PRESCHOOL

Learning Letters offers comprehensive instruction and practice in following directions, recognizing and writing upper- and lowercase letters, and beginning phonics. Math Readiness features activities that teach such important skills as counting, identifying numbers, creating patterns, and recognizing "same and different." Basic Concepts and Skills offers exercises that help preschoolers identify colors, read and write words, identify simple shapes, and more. 160 pages.

TITLE	ISBN	PRICE
Learning Letters	1-57768-329-3	$8.95
Math Readiness	1-57768-339-0	$8.95
Basic Concepts and Skills	1-57768-349-8	$8.95